MW01089969

UNDERSTANDING AND USING

English Grammar

FIFTH EDITION
WORKBOOK
VOLUME B

Betty S. Azar
Stacy A. Hagen
Geneva Tesh
Rachel Spack Koch

Understanding and Using English Grammar, Fifth Edition
Workbook, Volume B

Copyright © 2017, 2009, 2000, 1992 by Pearson Education, Inc.
All rights reserved.

No part of this publication may be reproduced,
stored in a retrieval system, or transmitted
in any form or by any means, electronic, mechanical,
photocopying, recording, or otherwise,
without the prior permission of the publisher.

Pearson Education, 221 River Street, Hoboken, NJ 07030

Azar Associates: Sue Van Etten, Manager

Staff credits: The people who made up the *Understanding and Using*
English Grammar Fifth Edition, Workbook team, representing content creation,
design, manufacturing, project management, publishing, rights management, and
testing, are Pietro Alongi, Rhea Banker, Stephanie Bullard, Warren Fischbach,
Nancy Flaggman, Gosia Jaros-White, Amy McCormick, Brian Panker,
Lindsay Richman, Robert Ruvo, Paula Van Ells, and Joseph Vella.

Contributing Editors: Jennifer McAliney, Janice Baillie

Text composition: Aptara

Illustrations: Don Martinetti–pages 148, 150 (bottom), 183, 207, 225; Chris Pavely–pages 135, 136,
137, 146, 150 (top), 153, 164, 170, 186, 191

Photo Credits—108: Shock/Fotolia; 117: Dolgachov/123RF; 118: Sam Spiro/Fotolia; 129: Aigarsr/
Fotolia; 139: Storergv/Fotolia; 151: Julief514/Fotolia; 159: Georgejmclittle/Fotolia; 170: Sushytska/
Fotolia; 176: Oksana Kuzmina/Fotolia; 188: Jan Wlodarczyk/Alamy Stock Photo; 201: Bonzami
Emmanuelle/Alamy Stock Photo.

ISBN 10: 0-13-427627-2
ISBN 13: 978-0-13-427627-4

Printed in the United States of America
1 0 2023

Contents

The titles listed below refer to section names, not practice titles. In general, one section has multiple exercises. The chart numbers refer to the grammar explanations in the *Understanding and Using English Grammar* Student Book.

Preface

The *Understanding and Using English Grammar Workbook* is a self-study textbook. It is keyed to the explanatory grammar charts found in *Understanding and Using English Grammar, Fifth Edition,* a classroom teaching text for English language learners, as well as in the accompanying *Chartbook,* a reference grammar with no exercises. Students can use the *Workbook* independently to enhance their understanding of English structures. Students can choose from a variety of exercises that will help them use English meaningfully and correctly.

This *Workbook* is also a resource for teachers who need exercise material for additional classwork, homework, testing, or individualized instruction.

The answers to the practices can be found in the *Answer Key* in the back of the *Workbook.* Its pages are perforated so that they can be detached to make a separate booklet. However, if teachers want to use the *Workbook* as a classroom teaching text, the *Answer Key* can be removed at the beginning of the term.

A special *Workbook* section called *Phrasal Verbs,* not available in the main text, is included in the *Appendix.* This section provides a reference list of common phrasal verbs along with a variety of exercises for independent practice.

CHAPTER 12
Noun Clauses

PRACTICE 1 ▶ Preview.
Read the passage. Underline the five noun clauses.

Patrick's Retirement

The fact that Patrick is retiring soon is not a secret. He has been teaching English at the community college for 35 years. He'll miss his students, but he's excited about his retirement. He's especially excited that he'll be able to travel more often. He told me that he's going to Greece this summer. I wonder what other countries he'll visit. I think that his wife is retiring soon too. We're having a retirement dinner for Patrick at his favorite restaurant next month. Everyone is invited to the dinner.

PRACTICE 2 ▶ Introduction. (Chart 12-1)
Underline the noun clauses. Some sentences don't have one.

1. I couldn't hear what he said.

2. What did he say?

3. I don't know what happened.

4. Why are you calling me?

5. I wonder why Dora is calling me.

6. Do you know who that man is?

7. Do you know where Hank lives?

8. What are they doing?

9. What they are doing is wrong.

10. What should I say?

11. I don't know what I should say.

12. Where will she live?

PRACTICE 3 ▶ Questions and noun clauses beginning with a question word. (Chart 12-2)
Complete the sentences with the given words.

1. they \ do \ want

   What ___*do they want*___ ?

2. want \ they \ what

   I don't know _____ .

3. Stacy \ live \ does

   Where _____?

4. lives \ where \ Stacy

   Can you tell me _____?

5. what \ Carl \ likes

   Do you know _____?

6. Carl \ does \ like

   What _____?

7. is \ Lina \ going

   Where _____?

8. is \ where \ going \ Lina

   I wonder _____.

PRACTICE 4 ▶ Questions and noun clauses beginning with a question word. (Chart 12-2)
Add punctuation and capitalization. Underline the noun clause if there is one.

1. Where does Lee live does he live downtown

   Where does Lee live? Does he live downtown?

2. I don't know where he lives

   I don't know <u>where he lives</u>.

3. What does Sandra want do you know

4. Do you know what Sandra wants

5. What Yoko knows is important to us

6. We talked about what Yoko knows

7. What do you think did you tell your professor what you think

8. My professor knows what I think

9. Where is the bus stop do you know where the bus stop is

10. What did he report what he reported is important

PRACTICE 5 ▶ Noun clauses beginning with a question word. (Chart 12-2)
Change each question in parentheses to a noun clause.

1. (*How far is it?*) I don't know ____*how far it is*____.

2. (*What is that on the table?*) I don't know _____.

3. (*How much did it cost?*) Ask her _____.

4. (*What did he say?*) _____ is very interesting.

5. (*When are they leaving?*) Do you know _____?

6. (*Which road should we take?*) Can you tell us _____?

7. (*Who called?*) Please tell me _____.

8. (*What's happening?*) Do you know _____?

9. (*Why do they work at night?*) Nobody knows _____.

10. (*What are they trying to do?*) _____ is difficult.

11. (*What kind of insects are these?*) I don't know _____ .

12. (*Whose keys are these?*) I wonder _____ .

PRACTICE 6 ▸ Questions and noun clauses beginning with a question word. (Chart 12-2)

Make questions with the given sentences. The words in parentheses are the answer to the question you make. Then change the question to a noun clause.

1. That man is (*Mr. Robertson*).

   QUESTION: _____*Who is that man?*_____

   NOUN CLAUSE: I want to know _____*who that man is.*_____

2. George lives (*in Los Angeles*).

   QUESTION: _____

   NOUN CLAUSE: I want to know _____

3. Ann bought (*a new dictionary*).

   QUESTION: _____

   NOUN CLAUSE: Do you know _____

4. It is (*350 miles*) to Denver from here.

   QUESTION: _____

   NOUN CLAUSE: I need to know _____

5. Jack was late for class (*because he missed the bus*).

   QUESTION: _____

   NOUN CLAUSE: The teacher wants to know _____

6. That is (*Tanya's*) phone.

   QUESTION: _____

   NOUN CLAUSE: Tom wants to know _____

7. Alex saw (*Ms. Frost*) at the meeting.

   QUESTION: _____

   NOUN CLAUSE: I don't know _____

8. (*Jack*) saw Ms. Frost at the meeting.

   QUESTION: _____

   NOUN CLAUSE: Do you know _____

9. Alice likes (*this*) book best, (*not that one*).

   QUESTION: _____

   Noun clause: I want to know _____

10. The plane is supposed to land (*at 7:14 P.M.*).

    QUESTION: _____

    NOUN CLAUSE: Could you tell me _____

PRACTICE 7 ▶ Noun clauses beginning with a question word. (Chart 12-2)
Complete each conversation with the correct phrase from the list. Write the letter.

a. what did he say
b. what he said
c. where are you going
d. where you are going

e. which bus should we take to the stadium
f. which bus we should take to the stadium
g. why did she do that
h. why she did that

1. A: What did the professor just say?

   B: I don't know _____. I couldn't understand anything.

2. A: Hey, Kim, _____?

   B: Downtown. We're going to the new show at the art museum.

3. A: Hello, there! You look lost. Can I help you?

   B: Yes, _____? We want to go to the football stadium in Fairfield.

4. A: Turn the TV up, please. I can't hear the weather reporter. Linda, _____?

   B: He said that there will be a lot of rain tomorrow.

5. A: Hello! Can you please tell us _____?

   B: Sorry, I don't know. I'm a stranger here myself.

6. A: I told you that we are going to Bermuda for a vacation, didn't I?

   B: Well, you told us about the vacation, but you didn't say _____.

7. A: Ms. Holsum just quit her job at the university.

   B: Oh, _____? That was such a good job!

   A: Nobody knows _____. It's a mystery.

PRACTICE 8 ▶ Noun clauses beginning with *whether* or *if*. (Chart 12-3)
Choose the correct completions.

1. We don't know _____.
   a. whether it will snow
   b. whether or not it will snow
   c. whether it will snow or not
   d. if it will snow
   e. if or not it will snow
   f. if it will snow or not

2. _____ doesn't matter to me.
   a. Whether or not it snows
   b. Whether it snows or not
   c. Whether does it snow or not
   d. If or not it snows
   e. If snows or not
   f. If does it snow

3. I wonder _____.
   a. whether or not does she know
   b. whether she knows or not
   c. whether does she know
   d. if does she know
   e. if she knows or not
   f. if or not she does know

PRACTICE 9 ▸ Review. (Charts 12-2 and 12-3)
Complete the questions using **Do you know**.

1. How much does this book cost? _____Do you know how much this book costs?_____

2. When is Flight 62 expected? _____

3. Where is the nearest restroom? _____

4. Is this word spelled correctly? _____

5. What time is it? _____

6. Is this information correct? _____

7. How much does it cost to fly from Toronto to London? _____

8. Where is the bus station? _____

9. Whose glasses are these? _____

10. Does this bus go downtown? _____

PRACTICE 10 ▸ Question words followed by infinitives. (Chart 12-4)
Complete each sentence in Column A with a phrase from Column B.

Column A

1. Where can I find fresh fish? I don't know __d__ .

2. Which person will be a better president?

   I don't know _____ .

3. Who can I get to repair the TV?

   I don't know _____ .

4. Should I get another job?

   I don't know _____ .

5. What's good to eat here?

   I don't know _____ .

6. Is the airport nearby?

   I don't know _____ .

7. What should it cost?

   I don't know _____ .

8. Do we need a lot of sandwiches for the party?

   I don't know _____ .

Column B

a. who to vote for

b. whether to look for one

c. how to fix it

✓ d. where to buy it

e. what to order

f. how many to prepare

g. how far it is from here

h. how much to spend

PRACTICE 11 ▸ Noun clauses beginning with *that*. (Chart 12-5)
Complete the sentences with the words in the box. More than one answer may be correct.

angry	confident	lucky	relieved
aware	disappointed	proud	worried

1. We are _____ that our son graduated with honors.

2. I am _____ that the store owner cheated me. That was awful!

3. Our teacher is _____ that all the students did poorly on the test. However, she is encouraging them to do well on the next test.

4. I was not _____ that our boss hired a new assistant. When did this happen?

5. It was _____ that we got off the elevator when we did. Just after we got off, it got stuck between floors, and the other passengers were inside for three hours!

6. Lee always wins the table tennis tournaments at our community center. He is _____ that he will win the one next weekend.

7. We were very _____ that the hurricane was coming our way. But it changed course and went out to sea instead. Now we are _____ that the hurricane didn't hit us.

PRACTICE 12 ▶ Noun clauses beginning with *that*. (Chart 12-5)
Rewrite the sentences in italics in two ways. Use the words from the original sentence.

1. *Nobody stopped to help Sam on the road. That is surprising.*
   a. It _____is surprising_____ that nobody stopped to help Sam on the road.
   b. The fact that ____nobody stopped to help Sam____ on the road ____is suprising.____.

2. *People in modern cities are distrustful of each other. That is unfortunate.*
   a. It _____ people in modern cities are distrustful of each other.
   b. That _____

3. *People in my hometown always help each other. That is still true.*
   a. It _____
   b. That _____

4. *People need each other and need to help each other. That is undeniably true.*
   a. It _____ people need each other and need to help each other.
   b. That _____ and need to help each other.

5. *People in cities often don't know their neighbors. That seems strange to me.*
   a. It _____ me _____ people in cities often don't know their neighbors.
   b. The fact that _____

PRACTICE 13 ▶ Quoted speech. (Chart 12-6)
Add punctuation and capitalization.

1. Millie said there's an important meeting at three o'clock

2. There's an important meeting at three o'clock she said

3. There is said Millie an important meeting at three o'clock

4. There is an important meeting today it's about the new rules said Millie

5. Where is the meeting Carl asked

6. Robert replied it's in the conference room

7. How long will it last asked Ali

8. I don't know how long it will last replied Millie

9. I'll be a little late said Robert I have another meeting until 3:00 P.M. today

10. Who is speaking at the meeting asked Robert

11. I am not sure who is speaking said Millie but you'd better be there everybody is supposed to be there

PRACTICE 14 ▸ Reported speech. (Chart 12-7)
Complete the sentences with the correct form of the verbs.

1. Tom said, "I am busy." Tom said that he _____was_____ busy.

2. Tom said, "I need some help." Tom said that he _____ some help.

3. Tom said, "I am having a good time." Tom said that he _____ a good time.

4. Tom said, "I have finished my work." Tom said that he _____ his work.

5. Tom said, "I finished it." Tom said that he _____ it.

6. Tom said, "Stay here." Tom told me _____ here.

PRACTICE 15 ▸ Reported speech. (Chart 12-7)
Change the quoted speech to reported speech. Pay attention to whether the reporting verb is past or present.

1. I asked Morgan, "Are you planning to enter law school?"

   I asked Morgan ___if / whether she was planning___ to enter law school.

2. Liam just asked me, "What time does the movie begin?"

   Liam wants to know _____.

3. Frank asked Carla, "Where have you been all afternoon?"

   Frank asked Carla _____ all afternoon.

4. Jaime just asked, "What is Kim's native language?"

   Jaime wants to know _____.

5. I asked myself, "Am I doing the right thing?"

   I wondered _____ the right thing.

6. Nancy asked, "Why didn't you call me?"

   Nancy wanted to know _____ her.

7. The teacher asked, "Have you been studying for the test?"

   The teacher asked us _____.

8. Rhonda asked Caroline, "Did you find your phone?"

   Rhonda asked Caroline _____.

PRACTICE 16 ▸ Reported speech with modal verbs. (Chart 12-8)
Complete the sentences with the correct form of the verbs.

1. Emily said, "I will arrive at noon." Emily said that she _____ at noon.

2. Emily said, "I am going to be there." Emily said that she _____ there.

3. Emily said, "I can solve that problem." Emily said that she _____ that problem.

4. Emily said, "I may come early." Emily said that she _____ early.

5. Emily said, "I might come early." Emily said that she _____ early.

6. Emily said, "I must leave at eight." Emily said that she _____ at eight.

7. Emily said, "I have to leave at eight." Emily said that she _____ at eight.

8. Emily said, "I should go to the library." Emily said that she _____ to the library.

PRACTICE 17 ▶ Reported speech with modal verbs. (Chart 12-8)

Change the quoted speech to reported speech. Pay attention to whether the reporting verb is past or present.

1. Jacob asked, "Can we still get tickets for the concert?"

   Jacob asked ___*if we could still get*_____ tickets for the concert.

2. Thomas said to us, "How can I help you?"

   Thomas wanted to know _____ us.

3. Eva asked, "Can you help me, Mario?"

   Eva asked Mario _____ her.

4. Charles said, "When will the final decision be made?"

   Charles wanted to know _____.

5. George asked me, "What time do I have to be at the lab in the morning?"

   George asked me _____ to be at the lab in the morning.

6. Yuki asked, "Who should I give this message to?"

   Yuki asked me _____ to.

7. The new student asked, "Where might I find an ATM?"

   The new student asked me _____ an ATM.

8. The impatient customer asked, "How long must I wait in line?"

   The impatient customer wanted to know _____ in line.

9. My son asked, "When are we going to get there?"

   My son asked me _____ there.

PRACTICE 18 ▶ Reported speech. (Charts 12-7 and 12-8)

Complete the sentences using the information in the conversation. Use past verb forms in the noun clauses if appropriate and possible.

CONVERSATION 1

"Where are you going, Ann?" I asked.

"I'm on my way to the farmers' market," she replied. "Do you want to come with me?"

"I'd like to, but I have to stay home. I have a lot of work to do."

"OK," Ann said. "Is there anything I can pick up for you?"

"How about a few bananas? And some apples if they're fresh?"

"Sure. I'd be happy to."

When I asked Ann where she _____, she said she _____
on her way to the farmer's market and _____ me to come with her. I said I
_____ to, but that I _____ to stay home because I _____
a lot of work to do. Ann kindly asked me if there _____ anything she _____
pick up for me at the market. I asked her to pick up a few bananas and some apples if they
_____ fresh. She said she'd be happy to.

CONVERSATION 2

"Where are you from?" asked the passenger sitting next to me on the plane.

"Chicago," I said.

"That's nice. I'm from Mapleton. It's a small town in northern Michigan. Have you heard of it?"

"Oh yes, I have," I said. "Michigan is a beautiful state. I've been there on vacation many times."

"Were you in Michigan on vacation this year?"

"No. I went far away from home this year. I went to India," I replied.

"Oh, that's nice. Is it a long drive from Chicago to India?" she asked me. My mouth fell open.
I didn't know how to respond. Some people certainly need to study geography.

The passenger sitting next to me on the plane _____ me where I _____ from.
I _____ her I _____ from Chicago. She _____ that she _____
from Mapleton, a small town in northern Michigan. She wondered if I _____ of
it, and I told her that I _____. I went on to say that I thought Michigan _____
a beautiful state and explained that I _____ there on vacation many times. She
_____ me if I _____ in Michigan on vacation this year. I replied
that I _____ and _____ her that I _____ far away, to
India. Then she asked me if it _____ a long drive from Chicago to India! My mouth fell
open. I didn't know how to respond. Some people certainly need to study geography.

PRACTICE 19 ▶ The subjunctive in noun clauses. (Chart 12-9)
Complete the sentences with the subjunctive form of the verbs in parentheses.

SITUATION: Jenny is taking her driving test next week.

  1. It is imperative that she (*arrive*) _____ at the test site on time.

  2. It is necessary that she (*provide*) _____ proof of insurance for her vehicle before
     the test begins.

  3. The Department of Motor Vehicles recommends that drivers (*get*) _____ plenty
     of practice before they take the driving test.

SITUATION: Joe is bored with his job.

  4. He has requested that he (*be*) _____ transferred to another department in his
     company.

  5. His boss suggested that he (*apply*) _____ for a promotion.

  6. His friend advised that he (*look*) _____ for a job with another company.

PRACTICE 20 ▶ Chapter review.

Part I. Choose the correct completions.

> ### Fitness Trackers
>
> Sherri has been exercising for a year, but she hasn't achieved the results she had hoped for. Her personal trainer at the gym suggested that she   gets / get   a fitness tracker. Fitness trackers have become very popular in recent years. These gadgets are usually worn as wristbands. A fitness tracker will count how many   steps Sherri takes / steps does Sherri take   in a day. Most fitness trackers will also measure how much sleep   she gets / does she get.   Some are able to calculate body weight and body mass. They can also show her what   is her heart rate / her heart rate is.   What makes fitness trackers popular is   whether / what   they help people keep track of their exercise routine. When people set fitness goals, it is often hard for them to know   if or not / whether or not   they have achieved it. A fitness tracker keeps a clear record.

Part II. Sherri is talking to Mark, a salesperson at a sporting goods store, about fitness trackers. Add punctuation to the conversation.

Can you help me find a fitness tracker Sherri asked

Mark replied Absolutely! What features are you looking for

I'm not sure Sherri said Can you tell me what is available

Sure he answered The basic trackers count your steps and monitor your sleep We also have more sophisticated models if you're looking for a heart rate monitor

I can't decide I think I need to take a look at them she said

Come this way, and I'll show you what we have

CHAPTER 13

Adjective Clauses

PRACTICE 1 ▸ Preview.
Read the passage. Underline the nine adjective clauses.

Advisors and Counselors

When students begin their university studies, they often feel overwhelmed. Most college campuses have several places where students can seek help. The first place that a new student should look for is the advising office. An academic advisor is someone who answers questions that are related to course selection, degree plans, and academic progress. Students usually meet with the same advisor over the course of their university education. The student and advisor develop a relationship in which the advisor serves as a mentor or guide. Another helpful place that students can turn to is the counseling office. A counselor is someone who helps students with personal issues that may or may not be related to the student's academic life. Counselors help students who have trouble with time management, test anxiety, career selection, or similar issues. Both advisors and counselors play an important role in student success.

PRACTICE 2 ▸ Adjective clause pronouns used as the subject. (Chart 13-1)
Underline the adjective clause in each sentence. Draw an arrow to the word it modifies.

1. We are looking for a person who fixes computers.

2. I know a man who lives on a boat.

3. In our office, there is a woman who speaks four languages.

4. There are several people who are bilingual in the office.

5. I work in an office that is in an old building.

6. The building that we work in was built in 1890.

7. Two trees that were over 200 years old were struck by lightning last night.

8. Two other trees which were nearby were not harmed.

9. The traffic jam was caused by one truck that had broken down.

10. The truck which caused the problem was in the middle of the highway.

PRACTICE 3 ▸ Adjective clause pronouns used as the subject. (Chart 13-1)
Choose the correct completions.

1. I thanked the woman _____ brought back our lost cat.
   a. who   b. that   c. which   d. she

2. The aquarium is looking for new employees _____ know a lot about dolphins.
   a. who   b. that   c. which   d. they

3. What is the TV channel _____ has stories about animals?
   a. who   b. it   c. which   d. that

4. On my flight, there was a weight-lifter _____ didn't fit into the airplane seat.
   a. who   b. that   c. he   d. which

5. None of the houses _____ have protective shutters were damaged in the typhoon.
   a. who   b. that   c. which   d. they

6. I'm transferring to a school _____ has a well-known program in cinematography.
   a. who   b. that   c. which   d. it

PRACTICE 4 ▸ Adjective clause pronouns as the object of a verb. (Chart 13-2)

Underline the adjective clause in each sentence. Draw an arrow to the word it modifies.

1. There's the man that I met last night.

2. There's the woman that Sandro is going to marry.

3. All the people whom we invited have accepted the invitation.

4. The book which I just read is going to be made into a movie.

5. I can't figure out how to use the software program that Jason installed.

6. We are still living in the house we built in 1987.

7. What happened to the cake I left on the table?

8. I bought the book my professor wrote.

PRACTICE 5 ▸ Adjective clause pronouns as the object of a verb. (Chart 13-2)

Choose the correct completions.

1. That's the woman _____ the people elected.
   a. who   b. whom   c. that   d. which   e. she   f. Ø

2. The man _____ the police arrested was not the thief.
   a. whom   b. he   c. that   d. which   e. who   f. Ø

3. I'd already seen the movie _____ we watched last night
   a. who   b. it   c. Ø   d. which   e. that   f. whom

4. Ms. McCarthy is a teacher _____ everyone loves.
   a. who   b. whom   c. Ø   d. which   e. that   f. her

5. Many of the people _____ we met on our vacation were very friendly.
   a. who   b. which   c. that   d. whom   e. Ø   f. they

6. A man _____ I know is going to be interviewed on a morning TV program.
   a. who   b. that   c. whom   d. which   e. him   f. Ø

PRACTICE 6 ▸ Adjective clause pronouns used as the subject or object of the verb. (Charts 13-1 and 13-2)

Complete the sentences with the correct adjective clause.

1. The book was good. I read it.

   The book that _____I read was good_____.

2. The movie was very sad. I saw it.

   The movie that _____.

3. Elephants are animals. They can live a long time.

   Elephants are animals that _____.

4. At the zoo, there were two fifty-year-old elephants. We photographed them.

   At the zoo, there were two fifty-year-old elephants which _____.

5. Sarah is a person. She does many things at the same time.

   Sarah is a person who _____.

6. Bill is a person. You can trust him.

   Bill is a person you _____.

7. The painting was valuable. The thieves stole it.

   The painting _____.

PRACTICE 7 ▸ Adjective clause pronouns used as the object of a preposition. (Chart 13-3)

Choose all possible completions.

1. The person _____ was Bob Jones in the customer service department.
   a. which I spoke to
   b. to which I spoke
   c. whom I spoke to
   d. to whom I spoke
   e. who I spoke to him
   f. to who I spoke
   g. that I spoke to
   h. to that I spoke
   i. I spoke to
   j. I spoke to him

2. This is the explanation _____.
   a. which I was referring to
   b. to which I was referring
   c. whom I was referring to
   d. to whom I was referring
   e. which I was referring to it
   f. that I was referring to
   g. to that I was referring
   h. I was referring to
   i. I was referring to it

PRACTICE 8 ▸ Adjective clauses. (Charts 13-1 → 13-3)

Write all the possible completions.

1. Mr. Green is the man
   | that |
   | who |
   | whom |
   | Ø |
   I was talking about.

2. She is the woman [   ] sits next to me in class.

3. The hat [   ] Tom is wearing is unusual.

4. Hunger and poverty are worldwide problems to [   ] solutions must be found.

5. I enjoyed talking with the man [____] I sat next to on the plane.

6. People [____] fear flying avoid traveling by plane.

7. The people about [____] the novelist wrote were factory workers and their families.

8. A barrel is a large container [____] is made of wood or metal.

PRACTICE 9 ▶ Adjective clauses. (Charts 13-1 → 13-3)

Correct the errors in the adjective clauses. Do not change any punctuation.

1. That's a subject I don't want to talk about it.

2. A person who he writes with his left hand is called a lefty.

3. Our family brought home a new kitten that we found it at the animal shelter.

4. What is the name of the podcast to that we listened last night?

5. The candidate for who you vote should be honest.

6. Here's a picture of Nancy who I took with my phone.

7. People have high cholesterol should watch their diets.

8. Suzie is going to marry the man she has always loved him.

9. There's an article in today's newspaper about a woman that she is 7 feet tall.

10. Passengers which have children may board the plane first.

PRACTICE 10 ▶ Whose vs. Who's. (Chart 13-4)

Choose the correct completions.

1. a. This class is for students _____ English needs improvement.
   a. who's   b. whose

   b. Belinda is a student _____ good in both math and languages.
   a. who's   b. whose

   c. Will the student _____ cell phone is ringing please turn it off?
   a. who's   b. whose

2. a. A customer _____ dissatisfied is not good for a business.
   a. who's   b. whose

   b. The customer _____ young son was crying tried to comfort him.
   a. who's   b. whose

3. a. Life is sometimes difficult for a child _____ parents are divorced.
   a. who's   b. whose

   b. I know a child _____ a chess prodigy.
   a. who's   b. whose

4. a. You should look for a doctor _____ right for you.
   a. who's   b. whose

   b. Do you know a doctor _____ office is close to campus?
   a. who's   b. whose

PRACTICE 11 ▸ Using *whose*. (Chart 13-4)
Combine the sentences into one using **whose**.

1. Do you know the man? His car is parked over there.
   _____

2. I know a skin doctor. His name is Dr. Skinner.
   _____

3. The people were very hospitable. We visited their home.
   _____

4. Mrs. Lake is the teacher. I enjoy her class the most.
   _____

5. The teacher asked the parents to confer with her. Their children were failing.
   _____

PRACTICE 12 ▸ Understanding adjective clauses. (Charts 13-1 and 13-4)
Check (✓) all the correct meanings for each sentence.

1. The secretary that trained my office assistant was arrested for ID theft.

   a. _____ My office assistant was arrested for ID theft.

   b. __✓__ A secretary trained my office assistant.

   c. __✓__ A secretary was arrested for ID theft.

2. The nurse who gave the patient her medication was unusually talkative.

   a. _____ The nurse was unusually talkative.

   b. _____ The patient was unusually talkative.

   c. _____ The patient received medication.

3. The taxi driver who turned in a lost wallet to the police received a large reward.

   a. _____ The taxi driver lost a wallet.

   b. _____ The police received a reward.

   c. _____ The taxi driver received a reward.

4. The math teacher whose methods include memorization and a focus on basic skills is very popular with parents.

   a. _____ The parents like the math teacher.

   b. _____ The parents focus on basic skills.

   c. _____ The math teacher requires memorization.

5. The computer that couldn't read your files had a virus.

    a. _____ The computer couldn't read your files.

    b. _____ The computer had a virus.

    c. _____ Your files had a virus.

6. A friend of mine whose husband is a firefighter accidentally started a fire in their kitchen.

    a. _____ My friend is a firefighter.

    b. _____ My friend started a fire.

    c. _____ The firefighter started a fire.

7. The surgeon who operated on my mother is undergoing surgery today.

    a. _____ The surgeon is having surgery today.

    b. _____ My mother is having surgery today.

    c. _____ My mother already had surgery.

PRACTICE 13 ▸ Using *where* in adjective clauses. (Chart 13-5)
Complete the sentences in two different ways with the given words.

1. grew up / in / I / which / where

    a. The town _____ has changed.

    b. The town _____ has changed.

2. I / which / lived / in / where

    a. The house _____ isn't there anymore.

    b. The house _____ isn't there anymore.

3. on / lived / which / where / I

    a. The street _____ is now a parking lot.

    b. The street _____ is now a parking lot.

4. where / which / I / played / in

    a. The park _____ is now a mall.

    b. The park _____ is now a mall.

PRACTICE 14 ▸ Using *when* in adjective clauses. (Chart 13-6)
Complete the sentences in three different ways with the given words.

1. on / which / when / I / go / that

    a. Saturday is the day _____ to the movies with my grandmother.

    b. Saturday is the day _____ to the movies with my grandmother.

    c. Saturday is the day _____ to the movies with my grandmother.

2. when / that / which / on / I play tennis

    a. Sunday is the day _____ with my friend.

    b. Sunday is the day _____ with my friend.

    c. Sunday is the day _____ with my friend.

PRACTICE 15 ▶ Using *where* and *when* in adjective clauses. (Charts 13-5 and 13-6)
Complete each conversation with the correct clause from the list. Write the letter.

    a. that George Washington slept in   e. where we can sit and talk
    b. when I spend time with my family   f. which I start my new job
    c. when they were really in love   g. which people here celebrate their independence
    d. where I was born   h. which you can do all the things you never could before

1. A: Where do you want to go after the movie?

   B: Let's go to a place _____ .

2. A: Sal and Lil broke up? That's impossible!

   B: There was a time _____ , but not anymore.

3. A: See you Monday!

   B: No. Don't you remember? Monday is the day on _____ .

4. A: Are you new in town?

   B: New? Are you kidding? This is the place _____ .

5. A: Is there something special about that house? It looks historic.

   B: Yes. They say it's a house _____ when he was on his way to Philadelphia.

6. A: Grandma is never home. Since she's retired, she's always doing something.

   B: Right. She says that retirement is the time in _____ .

7. A: What's the celebration here? Is it a holiday?

   B: Yes. It's the day on _____ .

8. A: Would you like to go out this weekend?

   B: No, thanks. Saturdays and Sundays are the days _____ .

PRACTICE 16 ▶ Adjective clauses. (Charts 13-1 → 13-6)
Choose all possible completions for each sentence.

1. Yoko told me about a student _____ has taken the entrance exam 13 times.
   a. who   b. whom   c. which   d. that

2. Is this the room _____ the meeting is going to be?
   a. which   b. where   c. that   d. Ø

3. Judge Savitt is a judge _____ people respect.
   a. whose   b. which   c. whom   d. Ø

4. I'll never forget the day _____ I met Bobbi.
   a. Ø   b. that   c. when   d. which

5. We're looking for a teacher _____ specialty is teaching dyslexic students.
   a. who   b. his   c. that   d. whose

6. I'm looking for an electric can opener _____ can also sharpen knives.
   a. who   b. which   c. that   d. Ø

7. The problems _____ Tony has seem insurmountable.
   a. what   b. whom   c. that   d. Ø

8. People _____ live in glass houses shouldn't throw stones.
   a. who   b. whom   c. which   d. Ø

PRACTICE 17 ▶ Using adjective clauses to modify pronouns. (Chart 13-7)

Complete the sentences in Column A with a clause from Column B.

Column A

1. May I ask you a question? There is something _____.

2. I don't have any more money. This is all _____.

3. Do you get the calculus homework?

   Anyone _____ must be a genius.

4. He's a spoiled child. His parents give him everything _____.

5. I'm sorry I can't help you. There's nothing _____.

Column B

a. who understands it

b. I can do

c. he wants

d. I want to know

e. that I have

PRACTICE 18 ▶ Punctuating adjective clauses. (Chart 13-8)

Add a comma to the adjective clauses that need one. Some adjectives clauses do not require commas.

1. I made an appointment with a doctor who is an expert on eye disorders.

2. I made an appointment with Dr. Raven who is an expert on eye disorders.

3. Bogotá which is the capital of Colombia is a cosmopolitan city.

4. The city that is the capital of Colombia is a large, cosmopolitan city.

5. South Beach which is clean, pleasant, and fun is known as a party town.

6. The person who writes the best essay will win a prize.

7. The first prize was given to Miranda Jones who wrote a touching essay about being an adopted child.

8. On our trip to Africa we visited Nairobi which is near several fascinating game reserves and then traveled to Egypt to see the pyramids.

9. To see wild animals, you have to fly to a city that is near a game reserve and then take a small plane to the reserve itself.

10. Someone who understands physics better than I do is going to have to help you.

11. Violent tropical storms that occur in western Asia are called typhoons.

12. Similar storms that occur on the Atlantic side of the Americas are called hurricanes rather than typhoons.

13. A typhoon which is a violent tropical storm can cause great destruction.

14. According to the news report, the typhoon that threatened to strike the Indonesian coast has moved away from land and toward open water.

15. Typhoon Haiyan which destroyed parts of Southeast Asia occurred in 2013.

PRACTICE 19 ▶ Punctuating adjective clauses. (Chart 13-8)

Choose the correct meaning for each sentence.

1. The students, who attend class five hours per day, have become quite proficient in their new language.
   a. All of the students attend class five hours per day.
   b. Some of the students attend class five hours per day.

2. The students who attend class five hours per day have become quite proficient in their new language.
   a. All of the students attend class five hours per day.
   b. Some of the students attend class five hours per day.

3. The orchestra conductor signaled the violinists, who were to begin playing.
   a. All of the violinists were to begin playing.
   b. Some of the violinists were to begin playing.

4. The orchestra conductor signaled the violinists who were to begin playing.
   a. All of the violinists were to begin playing.
   b. Some of the violinists were to begin playing.

5. I put the vase on the bookshelf, which is in the living room.
   a. I have more than one bookshelf.
   b. I have only one bookshelf.

6. I put the vase on the bookshelf that is in the living room.
   a. I have more than one bookshelf.
   b. I have only one bookshelf.

7. Trees which lose their leaves in winter are called deciduous trees.
   a. All trees lose their leaves in winter.
   b. Some trees lose their leaves in winter.

8. Pine trees, which are evergreen, grow well in a cold climate.
   a. All pine trees are evergreen.
   b. Some pine trees are evergreen.

PRACTICE 20 ▸ Using expressions of quantity in adjective clauses. (Chart 13-9)
Combine the sentences. Use the second sentence as an adjective clause. Add commas as necessary.

1. I received two job offers. I accepted neither of them.

   _____I received two job offers, neither of which I accepted._____

2. I have three brothers. Two of them are professional athletes.

   _____

3. Jerry is engaged in several business ventures. Only one of them is profitable.

   _____

4. The two women have almost completed law school. Both of them began their studies at age 40.

   _____

5. Eric is proud of his success. Much of it has been due to hard work, but some of it has been due to good luck.

   _____

6. We ordered an extra-large pizza. Half of it contained meat and half of it didn't.

   _____

7. The scientist won the Nobel Prize for his groundbreaking work. Most of his work was on genomes.

   _____

8. The audience gave a tremendous ovation to the Nobel Prize winners. Most of them were scientists.

   _____

PRACTICE 21 ▸ Using *which* to modify a whole sentence. (Chart 13-10)
Combine the sentences. Include an adjective clause that begins with ***which*** in the new sentence.

1. Mike was accepted at the state university. This is surprising.

   _____

2. Mike did not do well in high school. This is unfortunate.

   _____

3. The university accepts a few students each year with a low grade-point average. This is lucky for Mike.

   _____

4. The university hopes to motivate these low-performing students. This is a fine idea.

   _____

5. Mike might actually be a college graduate one day. This would be a wonderful!

   _____

PRACTICE 22 ▸ Reducing adjective clauses to adjective phrases. (Chart 13-11)
Change the adjective clauses to adjective phrases. Cross out the adjective clause and write the adjective phrase above it.

1. Do you see that man ~~who is wearing a green hat~~?   *wearing a green hat*
2. The person who is in charge of this department is out to lunch.
3. The picture which was painted by Picasso is extremely valuable.
4. The professors who are doing research will not teach classes next year.
5. The students' research projects which are in progress must be finished by the end of the year.
6. The students' research projects which are scheduled to begin in September will have to be completed by the middle of next year.
7. Toronto, which is the largest city in Canada, is not the capital.
8. In our solar system, there are eight planets that orbit the sun.
9. Pluto, which was formerly known as a planet, was reclassified as a dwarf planet in 2006.
10. Now there is a slang verb, *to pluto,* which means "to devalue someone or something."

PRACTICE 23 ▸ Reducing adjective clauses to adjective phrases. (Chart 13-11)
Combine the sentences. Use the second sentence as an adjective phrase. Add commas as necessary.

1. Brasilia is the capital of Brazil. It was officially inaugurated in 1960.
   Brasilia, officially inaugurated in 1960, is the capital of Brazil.

2. Rio de Janeiro used to be its capital. It is the second largest city in Brazil.

   _____

3. Two languages, Finnish and Swedish, are spoken in Helsinki. It is the capital of Finland.

   _____

4. In Canada, you see signs. They are written in both English and French.

   _____

5. Libya is a leading producer of oil. It is a country in North Africa.

_____

6. Simon Bolivar led the fight for independence early in the nineteenth century. He was a great South American general.

_____

7. Five South American countries are Venezuela, Colombia, Ecuador, Panama, and Peru. They were liberated by Bolivar.

_____

8. We need someone to design this project. He or she holds a degree in electrical engineering.

_____

9. The project will be finished next year. It is being built in Beijing.

_____

10. A lot of new buildings were constructed in Beijing in 2008. Beijing was the site of the summer Olympics that year.

_____

PRACTICE 24 ▶ Chapter review.

All of the following sentences contain one or two errors in adjective clauses, adjective phrases, or punctuation. Correct the errors using a correct adjective clause or adjective phrase, and the correct punctuation.

1. When we walked past the theater, we saw a lot of people waited in a long line outside the box office.
2. Students who living on campus are close to their classrooms and the library.
3. If you need any information, see the librarian sits at the central desk on the main floor.
4. My best friend is Anna who her birthday is the same day as mine.
5. Hiroko was born in Sapporo that is a city in Japan.
6. Patrick who is my oldest brother. He is married and has one child.
7. The person sits next to me is someone I've never met him.
8. My favorite place in the world is a small city is located on the southern coast of Thailand.
9. Dr. Darnell was the only person to that I wanted to speak.
10. Yermek whom is from Kazakhstan teaches Russian classes at the college.
11. The people who we met them on our trip last May are going to visit us in October.
12. Dianne Baxter that used to teach Spanish has organized a tour of Central America for senior citizens.
13. I've met many people since I came here who some of them are from my country.
14. People can speak English can be understood in many countries.
15. Grandpa is getting married again. This is a big surprise.

Gerunds and Infinitives, Part 1

PRACTICE 1 ▸ Introduction. (Chart 14-1)

Read the passage. <u>Underline</u> the six gerunds. Circle the eight infinitives.

Geochaching

Geocaching has become a popular outdoor activity in recent years. A geocache is a small container that someone has hidden outside. Participants use a GPS or a mobile device to find or hide geocaches. There are millions of geocaches around the world.

Ray and Isabel are looking for a geocache that someone has hidden. GPS coordinates have been posted on a website. Websites suggest leaving clues in addition to the coordinates, so Ray and Isabel are also using clues.

The geocache contains a logbook for signing and dating. Some participants like to place a small trinket or toy in the geocache. After Ray and Isabel find the geocache, they will sign the logbook. Then they need to place the geocache back exactly where they found it.

Ray and Isabel enjoy finding these hidden surprises, but they aren't having much luck today. They have been looking for over an hour, but they can't seem to find it. Ray wants to quit. He's tired and hungry. Isabel prefers to continue searching. She doesn't like to give up!

PRACTICE 2 ▸ Common verbs followed by gerunds. (Chart 14-2)

Complete the sentences with the gerund form of the verbs in the box.

argue	have	play	sell
drive	pay	read	smoke

1. Boris's hobby is chess. He enjoys _____ chess.

2. Leon's asthma is better now. He is breathing easier since he quit _____ a year ago.

3. I don't mind _____ an hour to work every day. I always listen to a good audio book in my car.

4. I put off _____ my taxes for too long; I missed the deadline and had to pay a penalty.

5. You should avoid _____ with your boss. Try to get along better.

6. Would you consider _____ your house at a lower price than you are asking?

7. Our teacher is so great! We really appreciate _____ a teacher like her.

8. When you finish _____ that book, may I borrow it?

PRACTICE 3 ▸ Common verbs followed by infinitives. (Chart 14-3)

Complete the sentences with the infinitive form of the verbs in the box.

arrive	fly	paint	transfer
cook	make	tell	work

1. Let's go to a restaurant. I don't want _____ tonight.

2. Ramzy doesn't go to school here any longer. He decided _____ to another school.

3. Scott has a terrible toothache. He needs _____ an appointment with a dentist.

4. Zach held out his arms and pretended _____ like a bird.

5. Reagan is a talented artist. She has offered _____ a picture of our family.

6. Caroline is graduating from law school this year. She plans _____ in a law firm next year.

7. Where's Jeff? He promised _____ on time today.

8. Jill seems upset. I've asked her what's wrong, but she refuses _____ me.

PRACTICE 4 ▸ Gerund or infinitive. (Charts 14-2 and 14-3)

Choose the correct completions.

1. William wants _____ us for dinner tonight.
   a. to join   b. joining

2. We offered _____ ice cream for all the kids.
   a. to buy   b. buying

3. I enjoy _____ large dishes of Indian food for my friends.
   a. to cook   b. cooking

4. Avoid _____ Highway 98. There's a lot of construction going on.
   a. to take   b. taking

5. Keep on _____! Sooner or later, you'll be able to finish the puzzle.
   a. to try   b. trying

6. Would you mind _____ up the heat? It's freezing in here.
   a. to turn   b. turning

7. I pretended _____ what Irv was saying, but in reality, I didn't understand a thing.
   a. to understand   b. understand

8. Phil seems _____ in a bad mood. Do you know why?
   a. to be   b. being

9. You should consider _____ this course. It's too hard for you.
   a. to drop   b. dropping

10. Because of the stormy weather, everyone was allowed _____ work early.
    a. to leave   b. leaving

11. Students are not permitted _____ their phones in class.
    a. to use   b. using

12. If you quit _____ coffee, you might sleep better.
    a. to drink   b. drinking

PRACTICE 5 ▸ Gerund or infinitive. (Charts 14-2 and 14-3)
Choose the correct completions.

1. John doesn't mind   to live / living   alone.
2. The traffic sign warns drivers   to be / being   careful on the slippery road.
3. Travelers are required   to show / showing   their IDs at the gate.
4. Don't delay   to make / making   your reservations. Book your travel now!
5. We expect the plane   to be / being   on time.
6. I certainly appreciate   to be / being   here! Thank you for inviting me.
7. Please stop   to hum / humming   that song over and over. It bothers me.
8. My doctor suggests   to exercise / exercising   for 30 minutes every day.
9. I was advised   to exercise / exercising   for 30 minutes every day by my doctor.
10. Jessica hopes   to graduate / graduating   next spring.

PRACTICE 6 ▸ Infinitives with objects. (Chart 14-4)
Choose all the possible completions for each sentence.

1. I want _____ that movie.
   a. to see   b. seeing   c. him to see
2. They told _____ them as soon as I got home.
   a. to call   b. calling   c. me to call
3. I expect _____ there early.
   a. to be   b. being   c. you to be
4. The police ordered _____ the building.
   a. not to enter   b. not entering   c. the people not to enter
5. We were asked _____ food and clothing for the hurricane victims.
   a. to contribute   b. contributing   c. them to contribute
6. Lisa expected _____ the lecture.
   a. to attend   b. attending   c. us to attend

PRACTICE 7 ▸ Infinitives with objects. (Chart 14-4)
Complete the sentences with **to work** or **me to work**. Write the correct completion(s). In some cases, both are possible.

1. She hoped _____*to work*_____ .
2. He ordered _____*me to work*_____ .
3. They wanted ___*to work / me to work*___ .
4. We agreed _____ .
5. She promised _____ .
6. They refused _____ .
7. He pretended _____ .
8. They didn't allow _____ .
9. You told _____ .
10. They would like _____ .
11. They expected _____ .
12. She decided _____ .
13. They needed _____ .
14. They required _____ .

PRACTICE 8 ▸ Gerund or infinitive. (Charts 14-2 → 14-4)

Complete the sentences with the gerund or infinitive form of the *italicized* verbs. Use **him** if an object is required.

Part I. Complete the sentences with *stay*.

1. I expect _____ .

2. I want _____ .

3. I forced _____ .

4. I invited _____ .

5. I considered _____ .

6. I told _____ .

7. I was told _____ .

8. I refused _____ .

9. I encouraged _____ .

10. I would like _____ .

Part II. Complete the sentences with *travel*.

1. He doesn't mind _____ .

2. He enjoys _____ .

3. He needed _____ .

4. He quit _____ .

5. He is allowed _____ .

6. He put off _____ .

7. He recommends _____ .

8. He can't stand _____ .

9. He finished _____ .

10. He mentioned _____ .

Part III. Complete the sentences with *work*.

1. They discussed _____ .

2. They intend _____ .

3. They were ordered _____ .

4. They decided _____ .

5. They offered _____ .

6. They delayed _____ .

7. They required _____ .

8. They hope _____ .

9. They plan _____ .

10. They avoided _____ .

PRACTICE 9 ▸ Common verbs followed by either gerunds or infinitives. (Chart 14-5)

Complete the sentences with the gerund or infinitive form of the verbs in parentheses.

1. a. Don't forget (*turn*) _____ off your computers before you leave the office.

   b. I'll never forget (*meet*) _____ the president when I was a child.

2. a. I'll remember (*stop*) _____ at the grocery store if I write myself a note and stick it in the window of my car.

   b. Do you remember (*see*) _____ a man running out of the bank with a large bag in his hand?

3. a. Don't give me any more advice. Please stop (*tell*) _____ me what to do.

   b. At the mall, I met my old English teacher. We stopped (*talk*) _____ for a while. That was very pleasant.

   c. I had a bad argument with my friend David two years ago. We stopped (*speak*) _____ then and haven't spoken since.

4. a. We regret (*buy*) _____ this house. It needs too many repairs.

   b. The letter said, "I regret (*tell*) _____ you that your application has been denied."

5. a. Mazzen tried very hard (*learn*) _____ Chinese, but he couldn't do it. He's just not good at languages.

   b. We don't know how to communicate with that man. We've tried (*talk*) _____ to him in Spanish, we've tried in Greek, we've tried in German, and we've tried in French. So far nothing's worked.

PRACTICE 10 ▸ Common verbs followed by either gerunds or infinitives. (Chart 14-5)
Choose the sentence that has the same meaning as the given sentence.

1. Jean and her husband stopped drinking coffee.
   a. They had a cup of coffee together.
   b. They don't drink coffee anymore.

2. I regret to inform you that your application has been denied.
   a. I am sorry to tell you that your application was not accepted.
   b. I am sorry I told you the news about your application.

3. Rita remembers locking the door this morning.
   a. Rita never forgets to lock the door in the morning.
   b. Rita remembers that she locked the door this morning.

4. I forgot to call my grandmother.
   a. I didn't call my grandmother.
   b. I don't remember whether I called my grandmother or not.

5. My back was sore from being at the computer all morning. I stopped to rest.
   a. I kept working.
   b. I took a break.

PRACTICE 11 ▸ Common verbs followed by either gerunds or infinitives. (Chart 14-5)
Choose the correct completions. In some sentences, both are correct.

1. It was raining hard, but we continued _____.
   a. to drive   b. driving

2. The veterinarian tried _____ the horse's life, but he failed.
   a. to save   b. saving

3. As soon as the play ended, the audience began _____ wildly.
   a. to applaud   b. applauding

4. I prefer _____ a movie rather than see one in a theater.
   a. to rent   b. renting

5. I prefer _____ movies at home.
   a. to see   b. seeing

6. I hate _____ in the house when the weather is beautiful.
   a. to stay   b. staying

7. I love _____ on the beach.
   a. to walk   b. walking

8. Most people enjoy _____ to music.
   a. to listen   b. listening

9. When you finish _____, call me and I'll come to pick you up.
   a. to shop   b. shopping

10. Please don't whine. I can't stand _____ you whine.
    a. to listen   b. listening to

PRACTICE 12 ▶ Using gerunds as the objects of prepositions. (Chart 14-6)
Complete the sentences with the gerund form of the verbs in the box.

buy	fly	hear	lower
drink	go	improve	take

1. Thank you for _____ care of my plants while I was in the hospital.

2. The kids are excited about _____ to the circus tomorrow.

3. Students who are interested in _____ their English conversation skills can sign up for special private classes.

4. Psychiatrists say that dreaming about _____ in the sky is quite common.

5. The candidate says he is committed to _____ taxes.

6. We are thinking about not _____ tickets for the opera this year. They have become so expensive.

7. I'm used to _____ tea with my meals. I never drink coffee.

8. We look forward to _____ from you soon.

PRACTICE 13 ▶ Using gerunds as the objects of prepositions. (Chart 14-6)
Choose the correct completions.

1. We are talking _____ opening a vegetarian restaurant in our neighborhood.
   a. to   b. about   c. with

2. Don't worry _____ being on time today. Everybody's going to be late because of the weather.
   a. to   b. about   c. with

3. Aren't you tired _____ studying? Let's take a break.
   a. with   b. about   c. of

4. Beth is a chocoholic. Nothing can stop her _____ eating chocolate whenever she feels like it.
   a. of   b. for   c. from

5. We are looking forward _____ seeing you again.
   a. to   b. of   c. from

6. Let's go dancing instead _____ going to the movies.
   a. with   b. about   c. of

7. Andy is still angry at me. He accused me _____ breaking his phone.
   a. of   b. for   c. in

8. He blames me _____ being too careless.
   a. of   b. about   c. for

9. I apologized _____ losing it, and I offered to replace it.
   a. of   b. in   c. for

10. Believe it or not, Andy is not interested _____ being my friend anymore.
   a. about   b. in   c. of

PRACTICE 14 ▶ Using gerunds as the objects of prepositions. (Chart 14-6)
Write the correct preposition and the correct form of the verbs in parentheses.

1. Henry is excited _____ (leave) _____ for India.

2. I have no excuse _____ (be) _____ late.

3. The rain prevented us _____ (complete) _____ the work.

4. Fred is always complaining _____ (have) _____ a headache.

5. Instead _____ (study) _____, Margaret went to a baseball game with some of her friends.

6. The weather is terrible tonight. I don't blame you _____ (want, not) _____ to go to the meeting.

7. Who is responsible _____ (wash) _____ and (dry) _____ the dishes after dinner?

8. The thief was accused _____ (steal) _____ a woman's purse.

9. I'm going to visit my family during the school vacation. I'm looking forward _____ (eat) _____ my mother's cooking and (sleep) _____ in my own bed.

10. I thanked my friend _____ (lend) _____ me lunch money.

PRACTICE 15 ▸ Using gerunds as the objects of prepositions. (Chart 14-6)

Complete each sentence with a preposition and a verb in the box. Write the verb in its gerund form.

answer	buy	clean	live	✓ take	write
arrive	change	fail	save	waste	

1. I'm thinking _____*about taking*_____ a class in digital photography.

2. Are you interested _____ a new computer?

3. Brrr! I don't like this cold weather. I'm used _____ in warmer climates.

4. Please forgive me (not) _____ your email until now. I've been very busy.

5. If you are worried _____ this class, why don't you get a tutor?

6. Everybody talks _____ the situation, but nobody does anything about it.

7. This room is a mess! Isn't anyone responsible _____ it up?

8. Bad weather prevented the plane _____ on time.

9. Thank you _____ a letter of recommendation for me.

10. The environmental group believes _____ energy. They want to stop people _____ electricity.

PRACTICE 16 ▸ Go + gerund. (Chart 14-7)

Look at the pictures of the activities that the Green family and the Evans family enjoy. Use expressions in Chart 14-7 to describe the activities. Write the correct tense of **go** + a gerund.

Part I. The Green family enjoys the outdoors.

1.   2.   3.   4.

1. Every weekend they _____ on the trails near their home.

2. In the summers they _____ on the lake. They like to go out in boats that have no motors.

3. In the winters they _____ in the mountains.

4. Last year they took a trip to Costa Rica, where they saw many
   colorful birds. They _____ .

5. On that trip, they also _____
   on a river.

5.

Part II. The Evans family enjoys different kinds of activities.

6.　　　　　　　7.　　　　　　　8.　　　　　　　9.

6. On Friday nights, they _____ at a social club near their home.

7. Every Monday night, they _____ at an alley at the mall.

8. Next year they are going on a tour of Europe, where they _____
   in five major cities. They'll see famous buildings, museums, and other landmarks.

9. Maybe they won't buy anything, but they _____ to see what's
   in the shops.

PRACTICE 17 ▸ Special expressions followed by -ing. (Chart 14-8)
Complete the sentences with the correct form of the verbs in the box.

do	lie	locate	look	play	watch

1. A: How was the picnic?

   B: Great! We had a lot of fun _____ volleyball on the beach.

2. A: What's the matter with Katy?

   B: She's very depressed. She spends all day _____ in bed, and she cries easily.

3. A: Oh, wow! You actually got in touch with Mr. Gordon, our twelfth-grade English teacher.

   B: Yes, I had a hard time _____ him, but I discovered that he was living in a
   retirement home.

4. A: George got fired? Really? Why?

   B: The boss caught him _____ through her private papers in her office.

5. A: Do you ever see Wilma these days?

   B: No. She spends all her time _____ research for her Ph.D.

6. A: Lillian doesn't let her children waste time _____ TV.

   B: Not all TV is bad. There are many good educational programs.

PRACTICE 18 ▸ *It* + infinitive; gerunds and infinitives as subjects. (Chart 14-9)
Choose the correct completions.

1. Is / It's   easy to use a computer.

2. Using a computer   is / it's   easy.

3. To speak another language   is / it's   not easy.

4. Is it / Is   difficult to speak another language?

5. Go / Going   dancing is fun.

6. It's / Is   fun to go dancing.

7. Traveling   is / it's   sometimes tiring.

8. It's dangerous   jump / to jump   out of airplanes in a parachute.

9. See / To see   the Grand Canyon is a thrilling experience.

10. Is / Is it   collecting coins an interesting hobby?

PRACTICE 19 ▸ Chapter review.
Complete the sentences with the correct form of the verbs in the box.

apply	end	operate	run	speak	use
camp	get	read	sleep	turn	watch

1. Our family goes _____ in the summer and fall. We love to cook outdoors and sleep in tents under the stars.

2. The doctor was forced _____ immediately to save the patient's life.

3. I have to drive more carefully. I can't risk _____ another speeding ticket.

4. Think about _____ for that new job. You can do it, I know.

5. The sign at the intersection warns drivers not _____ right when the light is red.

6. When Beth entered the room, she found her two cats _____ on her bed.

7. When you get through _____ the newspaper, could you please give me a little help in the kitchen?

8. I was furious at Bill's rude behavior. I threatened _____ our friendship.

9. Bill regretted _____ rude language and apologized for _____ to me in the way that he did.

10. The customers at the bank just stood _____ helplessly as a masked gunman held everyone at gunpoint.

11. But two police officers caught the gunman _____ out of the bank carrying two large bags of money.

PRACTICE 20 ▶ Chapter review.

Correct the errors. All the errors are in the use of gerunds and infinitives and the words that go with them.

Exercising the Brain

1. It's important keep your mind active.

2. Watch TV is not good brain exercise.

3. I prefer to spend time to play board games and computer games.

4. There is some evidence that older people can avoid to become senile by exercise their brain.

5. Playing word games it is one good way to stimulate your brain.

6. In addition, is beneficial for everyone to exercise regularly.

7. Physical exercise helps the brain by increase the flow of blood and deliver more oxygen to the brain.

8. Some studies show that to eat any type of fish just once a week increases brain health.

9. Doctors advise older people eating fish two or three times a week.

10. Everyone should try keep a healthy brain.

PRACTICE 21 ▶ Chapter review.

Correct the errors. All the errors are in the use of gerunds and infinitives and the words that go with them.

Studying Abroad

1. Pedro is interested to learn about other cultures.

2. He has always wanted studying abroad.

3. He had difficulty to decide where to study.

4. He has finally decided to living in Japan next year.

5. He's excited about attend a university there.

6. Right now he is struggling learning Japanese.

7. He has a hard time to pronounce the words.

8. He keeps on to study and to practice.

9. At night, he lies in bed to listen to Japanese language-teaching programs.

10. Then he dreams to travel to Japan.

CHAPTER 15

Gerunds and Infinitives, Part 2

PRACTICE 1 ▶ Preview.

Read the passage. Choose the correct completions. In some sentences, both choices are correct.

Life Hacks

Life hack is a term that is used for any trick or shortcut that people use in order   to be / being   more productive and efficient. There are several life hacks related to cleaning. For example, if you have food residue in a microwave that is too difficult   to remove / to be removed,   you can try   to place / placing   a small bowl or cup of water in the microwave and heating it for a couple of minutes. The steam from the water makes the old food   loosen up / to loosen up.   Afterwards, it is easy to wipe the microwave clean. There's a similar trick for blenders and food processors that need   cleaning / to be cleaned.   It takes a lot of time   to scrub / for scrubbing   a blender clean.   Running / To run   the blender with hot soapy water for about a minute beforehand will make it very easy to clean. Life hacks are simple solutions to everyday problems. They help us   to manage / manage   our time more efficiently.

PRACTICE 2 ▶ Infinitive of purpose: *in order to.* (Chart 15-1)

Choose the correct completions. In some sentences, both choices are correct.

1. Emily likes ＿＿＿ ice skating every weekend.
   a. to go
   b. in order to go

2. Darcy opened the door ＿＿＿ some fresh air in.
   a. to let
   b. in order to let

3. Beth practices night and day ＿＿＿ ready for her piano recital next month.
   a. to be
   b. in order to be

4. Susie sent me an email ＿＿＿ me that the meeting had been canceled.
   a. to inform
   b. in order to inform

5. We've decided not ＿＿＿ a vacation this year.
   a. to take
   b. in order to take

6. Did you remember ＿＿＿ Mr. Johnson?
   a. to call
   b. in order to call

7. On nice summer nights, we often walk on the beach ＿＿＿ the sunsets.
   a. to watch
   b. in order to watch

8. The boys were so noisy that I had to ring a loud bell ＿＿＿ their attention.
   a. to get
   b. in order to get

9. Airport workers wear ear protectors ＿＿＿ their ears from jet noise.
   a. to protect
   b. in order to protect

10. I need ＿＿＿ for my grammar test.
    a. to study
    b. in order to study

PRACTICE 3 ▸ Infinitive of purpose: *in order to.* (Chart 15-1)
Complete the sentences with *to* or *for*.

David is in Mexico ...

1. visit.

2. a visit.

3. a convention.

4. his cousin's wedding.

5. go sightseeing.

6. learn Spanish.

7. his health.

8. see the Mayan ruins.

9. the cool mountain air.

PRACTICE 4 ▸ Adjectives followed by infinitives. (Chart 15-2)
Complete each conversation with the correct phrase from the list. Write the letter.

a. to hear that
b. to bring the paper cups and paper plates
c. to get into one
d. to be alive
e. to introduce our country's president
f. to lose the next game

1. A: Marta had a bad accident, I heard.

   B: Yes, she did. She's lucky _____ .

2. A: Why does Mr. Carlin walk up 12 flights of stairs every day? Is it for the exercise?

   B: No, not at all. He has a phobia about elevators. He's afraid _____ .

3. A: Who is going to cook dinner for our next meeting?

   B: I can't cook, but I'm willing _____ .

4. A: Our dog died.

   B: Oh, that's a shame. I'm very sorry _____ .

5. A: Our three best soccer players are out with injuries.

   B: I know. Without them, you're likely _____ .

6. A: Turn the volume up. I want to hear what the senator is saying.

   B: "Ladies and gentlemen, I am proud _____ ."

PRACTICE 5 ▸ Using infinitives with *too* and *enough.* (Chart 15-3)
Complete the sentences with *too* or *enough*.

1. John dropped his physics course because it was _____ difficult for him.

2. We'd like to go out in our sailboat today, but there isn't _____ wind to sail.

3. I think it's _____ late to get tickets to the concert. I heard they were sold out.

4. Peter has turned 20. Now he's _____ old to take part in the ski races for teenagers.

5. It's _____ hot to take my daily walk. I'm staying inside.

6. It's hot _____ to fry an egg on the sidewalk!

7. Professor Andrews is always interesting, but I'm _____ tired to go to the lecture tonight.

8. I need to work on my essay all weekend. I barely have _____ time to finish it.

9. Ramzy just turned 13 years old. Do you think he's old _____ to take scuba diving lessons?

10. Hannah is _____ young to understand. She'll understand when she's older.

11. I'm _____ sleepy to watch the rest of the TV movie. Let me know how it turns out in the end.

12. These new windows are made of specially treated glass. It's strong _____ to resist the strong winds of hurricanes.

13. It's _____ dark to see in here. Please turn on the lights.

14. There's not _____ light in here. Can you turn on another light?

15. A trip to Europe is _____ expensive for our family this year. We don't have _____ money to travel this year.

16. You're _____ young to drive a car, Emily. You're only 12 years old! There will be time _____ to drive when you're older.

PRACTICE 6 ▸ Using infinitives with *too* and *enough*. (Chart 15-3)
Choose the correct statement for each situation. In some cases, both answers are correct.

1. Karen has been saving up for an electric car. She went to the car dealership today. She has more than enough money to buy a gasoline car, but she needs to save a little more for an electric car.
   a. An electric car is too expensive for Karen to buy.
   b. Karen has enough money to buy an electric car.

2. Ben wants to apply for a position as a web developer at the university. The job requires a bachelor's degree and five years of experience. Ben has a bachelor's degree, but he has only worked as a web developer for two years.
   a. He does not have enough experience for the position.
   b. He is too inexperienced for the position.

3. I went to an excellent presentation last night. The huge auditorium was completely filled with people who were excited to see the popular speaker. I had to sit in the very back, but I was still able to hear every word.
   a. The speaker was too loud.
   b. The speaker was loud enough.

4. Harry wants to run in the Boston Marathon. He has to be able to run a marathon in three hours and forty seconds in order to qualify for the race. Harry can run a marathon in three hours and twenty-five seconds.
   a. He is fast enough to qualify for the race.
   b. He is too slow to qualify for the race.

PRACTICE 7 ▸ Passive infinitives and gerunds: present. (Chart 15-4)
Complete the sentences with the passive form of the verbs in parentheses.

1. I hope (*accepted*) _____ at State College.

2. I would like (*given*) _____ a scholarship.

3. Leo wants (*picked*) _____ for the soccer team.

4. Cats enjoy (*petted*) _____ .

5. Babies need (*held*) _____.

6. I really appreciate (*asked*) _____ to join this group.

7. Daniel is shy. He avoids (*noticed*) _____.

8. Annie mentioned (*invited*) _____ to a party at her boss's house.

9. I can't go out tonight. My essay needs (*finished*) _____ by tomorrow morning.

10. Your essay was supposed (*submitted*) _____ yesterday. You missed the deadline.

PRACTICE 8 ▶ Passive infinitives and gerunds: present. (Chart 15-4)
Choose the correct completions.

1. The mail is supposed _____ before noon.
   a. to deliver   b. to be delivered

2. The mail carrier is supposed _____ the mail before noon.
   a. to deliver   b. to be delivered

3. Janice is going to fill out an application. She wants _____ for the job.
   a. to consider   b. to be considered

4. I expect _____ at the airport by my uncle.
   a. to meet   b. to be met

5. Mr. Steinberg offered _____ us to the train station.
   a. to drive   b. to be driven

6. The kids appear _____ about the trip.
   a. to excite   b. to be excited

7. My co-worker and I agreed _____ the work equally.
   a. to divide   b. to be divided

8. Our boss appears _____ with this arrangement.
   a. to please   b. to be pleased

PRACTICE 9 ▶ Passive infinitives and gerunds: present. (Chart 15-4)
Choose the correct completions.

1. Shhh! Don't ask questions! The professor doesn't appreciate _____ when he's speaking.
   a. interrupting   b. being interrupted

2. Avoid _____ Highway 77. There are a lot of delays because of construction.
   a. taking   b. being taken

3. The mountain climbers are in danger of _____ by an avalanche.
   a. killing   b. being killed

4. Does Dr. Johnson mind _____ at home if his patients need his help?
   a. calling   b. being called

5. I'm interested in _____ my conversational skills.
   a. improving   b. being improved

6. When Alex got home from school, he didn't mention _____ by his teacher.
   a. scolding   b. being scolded

7. Sally's low test scores kept her from _____ to the university.
   a. admitting   b. being admitted

8. Mr. Miller gave no indication of _____ his mind.
   a. changing   b. being changed

PRACTICE 10 ▸ Passive infinitives and gerunds: present. (Chart 15-4)
Complete the sentences with the correct form of the verbs in parentheses.

1. We turn off the phone during dinner. We don't want (call) _____ at that time.

2. Not many people enjoy (call) _____ by salespeople.

3. I need (call) _____ the credit card company. I think there's a mistake on my bill.

4. Each candidate hopes (elect) _____ by a large majority of the people.

5. It's not easy (elect) _____ .

6. Our mayor has an excellent chance of (re-elect) _____ .

7. Some people want (elect) _____ a new mayor.

8. Sometimes teenagers complain about not (understand) _____ by their parents.

9. Many parents try (understand) _____ their teenage children.

10. Some parents get tired of (try) _____ to understand their teenagers.

11. Sometimes teenagers would like just (leave) _____ alone.

PRACTICE 11 ▸ Past forms of infinitives and gerunds. (Chart 15-5)
Choose the correct completions. More than one answer may be correct.

1. Scott didn't finish his reading homework. When he got to class, he pretended _____ the assignment.
   a. to have read
   b. reading
   c. having read
   d. having been read

2. I would like _____ the Statue of Liberty when I was in New York, but I didn't have time.
   a. to visit
   b. visiting
   c. to have visited
   d. having been visited

3. Lily is worried about _____ her driver's license. She doesn't want to be a victim of identity theft.
   a. to lose
   b. losing
   c. having lost
   d. to have lost

4. I'm honored _____ as a candidate.
   a. to have chosen
   b. to be chosen
   c. to have been chosen
   d. being chosen

5. Rhonda regrets _____ to a small town. She misses all the conveniences of the city.
   a. to move
   b. having moved
   c. to have moved
   d. moving

6. Carlos was an outstanding student. Dr. Clement was happy _____ a letter of recommendation for him.
   a. writing
   b. being written
   c. to have written
   d. to write

7. You mentioned _____ to Nepal. Did you enjoy your trip?
   a. traveling
   b. having traveled
   c. to have traveled
   d. to travel

8. Maya was very disappointed. She was expecting _____ a scholarship.
   a. to receive
   b. to be received
   c. to have received
   d. to have been received

9. Is Gavin OK? He appeared _____ very sick yesterday.
   a. having been
   b. being
   c. to be
   d. to have been

PRACTICE 12 ▸ Using gerunds or passive infinitives following *need*. (Chart 15-6)
Choose all of the sentences that can follow the given sentence.

1. A lot of things in our house don't work.
   a. We need to repair them.
   b. They need to repair.
   c. They need to be repaired.
   d. They need repairing.

2. The refrigerator is so old that it hardly works anymore.
   a. We need to replace the refrigerator.
   b. It needs to replace.
   c. It needs to be replaced.
   d. It needs replacing.

3. The sink has been leaking for a month.
   a. A plumber needs to fix the sink.
   b. The sink needs fixing.
   c. The sink needs to be fixed.
   d. The sink needs to fix.

4. The color of the walls has faded.
   a. We need to paint the walls.
   b. The walls need to be painted.
   c. The walls need to paint.
   d. The walls need painting.

5. We don't have a good repair person.
   a. We need to find a good repair person.
   b. A good repair person needs to find.
   c. A good repair person needs to be found.
   d. We need a repair person to find.

6. Please tell your repair person to call me.
   a. I need to call your repair person.
   b. I need to be called by your repair person.
   c. Your repair person needs to call me.
   d. Your repair person needs calling.

PRACTICE 13 ▶ Using verbs of perception. (Chart 15-7)

Complete the sentences with a verb in the box. Use each word only once. Use the simple form or the *-ing* form, whichever seems better to you. Sometimes both are OK.

arrive	do	pass	reach	talk
cry	leave	practice	rock	win

1. Whenever I can, I like to watch the basketball team _____ for the upcoming game.

2. It's interesting to sit in the airport and watch all the people _____ by.

3. I heard an upset baby _____ .

4. Did you see Charles _____ the office? He ran out in a really big hurry.

5. It was a thrill to see my brother _____ the chess tournament last year.

6. I was amazed to see the police _____ so soon after my call.

7. I can't stand to be on a boat. When I feel the boat _____ , I get seasick.

8. When I watch my yoga instructor _____ the exercises, it seems easy, but when I try them, it is hard.

9. We listened to the newscaster _____ about rising prices.

10. A security guard at the bank observed a suspicious-looking man _____ into his pocket for something. The guard thought it was a gun, but it turned out to be the man's asthma inhaler.

PRACTICE 14 ▶ Using the simple form after *let* and *help*. (Chart 15-8)

Choose the correct completions. More than one completion may be correct.

1. The school guard stopped all the traffic to let the children _____ the street.
   a. cross   b. to cross   c. crossing

2. My friend Ole is very relaxed. He never lets anything _____ him.
   a. to bother   b. bother   c. bothering

3. My daughter helped me _____ an application online.
   a. filling out   b. filled out   c. fill out

4. Will you please help me _____ the kitchen? Otherwise, I'll be here all night!
   a. clean up   b. to clean up   c. cleaning up

5. Elsa used to have very short hair, but now it is longer. She is letting it _____.
   a. growing   b. to grow   c. grow

6. We don't let our dog _____ around outside. We always take him for walks on a leash.
   a. run   b. to run   c. running

7. Is it true that if you eat fish every day, it will help you _____ smarter?
   a. to become   b. becoming   c. become

8. Did someone help you _____ this research paper?
   a. write   b. wrote   c. writing

PRACTICE 15 ▸ Using causative verbs: *make, have, get.* (Chart 15-9)
Complete the sentences with the correct form of the verbs in parentheses.

1. The general made the soldiers (*stand*) _____ at attention.

2. Don't get rid of those shoes just because they are old. Have them (*fix*) _____ at the shoe repair shop.

3. Exercise makes your heart (*beat*) _____ faster.

4. What can we do to get Marissa (*stop*) _____ smoking?

5. Jean finally got her son (*clean*) _____ his room.

6. Paula's new haircut makes her (*look*) _____ ten years younger.

7. I'm sorry, sir. Your prescription has expired. Have your physician (*call*) _____ us here at the pharmacy, and then we can refill it for you.

8. Please take this document to the copy store and have 15 copies (*make*) _____. There are 150 pages, so you'd better have spiral bindings (*put*) _____ on too.

PRACTICE 16 ▸ Using causative verbs: *make, have, get.* (Chart 15-9)
Choose the correct completions. More than one completion may be correct.

1. You can _____ the company credit your account when you return the shoes.
   a. make   b. have   c. get

2. If you're nice to James, maybe you can _____ him to drive you to the airport.
   a. make   b. have   c. get

3. I'll _____ the taxi driver take me to the airport.
   a. make   b. have   c. get

4. The comedian is so funny. I can't help laughing even though I'm sad. That comedian can _____ anyone laugh.
   a. make   b. have   c. get

5. The students tried to _____ the professor to postpone the exam, but he didn't.
   a. make   b. have   c. get

6. I'm going to _____ my car washed on Saturday.
   a. make   b. have   c. get

7. Ms. Andrews isn't there? _____ her call me, please.
   a. Make   b. Have   c. Get

8. You don't have to go to the party. No one can _____ you go.
   a. make   b. have   c. get

PRACTICE 17 ▸ Using a possessive to modify a gerund. (Chart 15-10)
Complete the sentences with the correct form of the *italicized* pronouns.

1. *you* a. FORMAL: I appreciate _____ taking time to meet with me today.

   b. INFORMAL: I appreciate _____ taking time to meet with me today.

2. *he* a. FORMAL: Every morning, Charlie takes a long shower and sings at the top of his lungs.

   I can't stand _____ singing in the shower.

   b. INFORMAL: I can't stand _____ singing in the shower.

3. *she*   a. FORMAL: Joy shouldn't be driving. I'm worried about _____ driving so soon after her eye surgery.

     b. INFORMAL: I'm worried about _____ driving so soon after her eye surgery.

4. *they*   a. FORMAL: Some students were trying to check their messages during class. The teacher insisted on _____ putting away all electronic devices.

     b. INFORMAL: The teacher insisted on _____ putting away all electronic devices.

5. *I*   a. FORMAL: My brother was annoyed by _____ borrowing his jacket without asking him first.

     b. INFORMAL: My brother was annoyed by _____ borrowing his jacket without asking him first.

6. *we*   a. FORMAL: I hope you don't mind _____ having to leave the party a little early.

     b. INFORMAL: I hope you don't mind _____ having to leave the party a little early.

PRACTICE 18 ▶ Verb form review. (Chapters 14 and 15)
Choose the correct completions.

1. I enjoy _____ to the park on summer evenings.
   a. to go   b. going   c. being gone   d. go

2. Don't forget _____ as soon as you arrive home.
   a. to call   b. calling   c. call   d. to be called

3. When we kept getting unwanted calls, I called the phone company and had my phone number _____.
   a. change   b. changed   c. to change   d. changing

4. Julie should seriously consider _____ an actress. She's a very talented performer.
   a. to become   b. become   c. becoming   d. will become

5. _____ TV is not recommended for young children.
   a. Watch   b. Being watched   c. Watching   d. To be watched

6. After their children had grown up, Mr. and Mrs. Sills decided _____ to a condominium in the city.
   a. moved   b. moving   c. move   d. to move

7. Are you interested in _____ the movie at University Theater?
   a. see   b. to see   c. being seen   d. seeing

8. The store manager caught the cashier _____ money from the cash register and promptly called the police. They discovered that it had been going on for a long time.
   a. to steal   b. stealing   c. stole   d. being stolen

9. The city authorities advised us _____ all drinking water during the emergency.
   a. to boil   b. to be boiled   c. boiling   d. boil

10. If we leave now for our trip, we can drive half the distance before we stop _____ lunch.
   a. having   b. to have   c. have   d. for having

11. It was difficult _____ the dialogue in the movie. The acoustics in the theater were very bad.
   a. to hear   b. hearing   c. heard   d. to heard

12. Our school basketball team won the championship game by _____ two points in the last five seconds. It was the most exciting game I have ever attended.
   a. being scored   b. to score   c. scoring   d. score

13. The flight attendants made all the passengers _____ their seat belts during the turbulence.
    a. to buckle   b. buckling   c. to buckled   d. buckle

14. At our class reunion, we had a lot of fun _____ at pictures of ourselves from 20 years ago.
    a. looking   b. look   c. looked   d. to look

15. It has become necessary _____ water in the metropolitan area because of the severe drought.
    a. rationing   b. ration   c. have rationed   d. to ration

16. Ethan got a bad grade on his first essay, but he seems _____ his lesson. He edits his work very carefully now.
    a. to have learned   b. having learned   c. learning   d. to have been learned

17. Scott is very upset about _____ his cell phone. It had hundreds of his family photos stored in it.
    a. having been lost   b. having lost   c. to have lost   d. to have been lost

18. I passed a terrible car accident on my way home. Several people appeared _____.
    a. to have injured   b. being injured   c. to injure   d. to have been injured

PRACTICE 19 ▸ Verb form review. (Chapters 14 and 15)

Complete the sentences with the correct form of the verbs in parentheses. Some sentences are passive.

1. Bill decided (buy) _____ a new car rather than a used one.

2. We delayed (open) _____ the doors of the testing center until exactly 9:00.

3. I really dislike (ask) _____ to answer questions in class when I haven't prepared my homework.

4. I certainly didn't anticipate (have) _____ to wait in line for three hours for tickets to the baseball game!

5. When I was younger, I used (wear) _____ mini-skirts and bright colors. Now I am accustomed to (dress) _____ more conservatively.

6. Skydivers must have nerves of steel. I can't imagine (jump) _____ out of a plane and (fall) _____ to the earth. What if the parachute doesn't open?

7. We are looking forward to (take) _____ on a tour of Athens by our Greek friends.

8. I told the mail carrier that we would be away for two weeks on vacation. I asked her (stop) _____ (deliver) _____ our mail until the 21st. She told me (fill) _____ out a form at the post office so that the post office would hold our mail until we returned.

9. The elderly man next door is just sitting in his rocking chair (gaze) _____ out the window. I wish there were something I could do (cheer) _____ him up.

10. I resent (have) _____ to work on this project with Fred. I know I'll end up with most of the work falling on my shoulders.

PRACTICE 20 ▸ Verb form review. (Chapters 14 and 15)

Choose the correct completions.

1. Alice didn't expect _____ to Bill's party.
   a. to ask   b. to be asked   c. asking

2. Matthew left the office without _____ anyone.
   a. tell   b. telling   c. told

3. It's useless. Give up. Enough's enough. Don't keep _____ your head against a brick wall.
   a. beat   b. beating   c. to beat

4. I hope _____ a scholarship for the coming semester.
   a. to award   b. to be awarded   c. being awarded

5. We are very pleased _____ your invitation.
   a. to accept   b. to be accepted   c. accept

6. It was exciting _____ to faraway places last year.
   a. travel   b. to travel   c. to traveled

7. Conscientious parents don't let their children _____ too much screen time.
   a. have   b. to have   c. having

8. Did you see that deer _____ across the road?
   a. run   b. ran   c. to run

9. Mr. Carson was very lucky _____ to represent the company in Paris.
   a. to be chosen   b. choosing   c. to chose

10. Last Saturday, we went _____.
    a. to shop   b. shopping   c. to shopping

11. _____ in the mountains is Tom's favorite activity.
    a. Hike   b. Hiking   c. Go to hike

12. The physical activity makes him _____ good.
    a. feel   b. to feel   c. feeling

13. Martha opened the window _____ in some fresh air.
    a. let   b. letting   c. to let

14. Scott wastes a lot of time _____ out with his friends at the mall.
    a. hanging   b. to hang   c. hang

15. Did you remember _____ the front door?
    a. lock   b. to lock   c. locking

16. I don't remember ever _____ that story before.
    a. hearing   b. heard   c. to hear

17. You should stop _____ if you get sleepy.
    a. drive   b. driving   c. to drive

18. I have trouble _____ asleep at night.
    a. fall   b. to fall   c. falling

19. After driving for three hours, we stopped _____ something to eat.
    a. to get   b. getting   c. got

20. The refrigerator needs _____ again.
    a. to be fixed   b. to fix   c. fixed

21. That pan is really hot. It's too hot _____ up without an oven mitt.
   a. pick
   b. picking
   c. to pick

22. Braden was annoyed _____ his driving test by only one question.
   a. to be failed
   b. to failed
   c. to have failed

23. Alyssa parked her car in a fire zone. Now her car is gone. It appears _____ .
   a. to have towed
   b. to have been towed
   c. having towed

24. Thank you for _____ honest.
   a. being
   b. been
   c. to be

25. I appreciate _____ the truth.
   a. to be told
   b. to have told
   c. having been told

PRACTICE 21 ▸ Verb form review. (Chapters 14 and 15)
Correct the errors.

1. You shouldn't let children playing with matches.

2. Maddie was lying in bed to cry.

3. You can get there more quickly by take River Road instead of the interstate highway.

4. Nathan expected being admitted to the university, but he wasn't.

5. Our lawyer advised us not signing the contract until she had a chance to study it very carefully.

6. John was responsible for to notify everyone about the meeting.

7. Apparently, he failed to calling several people.

8. I couldn't understand what the reading said, so I asked my friend translated it for me.

9. You can find out the meaning of the word by look it up in a dictionary.

10. No, that's not what I meant to say. How can I make you understanding?

11. Serena wore a large hat for protect her face from the sun.

12. We like to go to fish on weekends.

13. Maybe you can get Charlie taking you to the airport.

14. My doctor advised me not eating food with a high fat content.

15. Doctors always advise eat less and exercising more.

16. Allen smelled something to burn. When he ran into the kitchen, he saw fire coming out of the oven.

17. The player appeared to have been injure during the basketball game.

18. David mentioned having been traveled to China last year.

CHAPTER 16

Coordinating Conjunctions

PRACTICE 1 ▶ Preview.

Read the passage. Complete the sentences.

Community Gardening

Gardening is a popular hobby. Some people have herb gardens with plants such as thyme, basil, mint, and oregano. These herbs are useful for seasoning food, brewing in tea, or making medicinal remedies. Other people grow vegetable gardens for food. Some people prefer to grow flower gardens. They enjoy the beauty and fragrance of their plants.

It is not easy for people who live in large cities to grow a garden. Not only do most city dwellers lack the space for a garden, many also lack the knowledge to plan and maintain a garden. One solution to this problem is a community garden. A community garden is a large piece of land that is gardened by several people. In some cases, everyone works together in one large garden. In other cases, each person has his or her own small garden plot.

There are several benefits to community gardens. These gardens give people who live in cities an opportunity to grow their own fresh vegetables and herbs; they offer people the chance to participate in a fun hobby; and they provide people with a sense of community and a connection to the environment.

---

1. Four examples of herbs are _____, _____, _____, and _____.

2. Three common uses for herbs are _____ food, _____ in tea, and _____ medicinal remedies.

3. Three types of gardens are _____, _____, and _____ gardens.

4. It might be difficult for people who live in large cities to grow a garden because they lack the _____ and _____ needed to grow a garden.

5. Four benefits of community gardens include having fresh _____ and _____, a fun _____, a sense of _____, and a _____ to the environment.

PRACTICE 2 ▸ Parallel structure. (Chart 16-1)

Choose the correct completions.

1. In the winter, Iceland is cold and _____.
   a. ice   b. dark   c. a country

2. Dan opened the door and _____ the room.
   a. enter   b. entering   c. entered

3. This dish is made of meat, potatoes, and _____.
   a. spicy   b. salty   c. vegetables

4. Lindsey was listening to music and _____ homework at the same time.
   a. does   b. doing   c. did

5. Mimi learned how to sing and _____ at the Academy of the Arts.
   a. danced   b. dancing   c. dance

6. I have written and _____ her, but I have received no response.
   a. call   b. calling   c. called

7. Somebody called and _____ up.
   a. hung   b. hang   c. hanging

8. Don't call and _____ up. Leave a short message.
   a. hung   b. hang   c. hanging

PRACTICE 3 ▸ Parallel structure. (Chart 16-1)

Circle the conjunction that joins the parallel words. Then <u>underline</u> the words that are parallel and choose the part of speech that describes them.

1. These apples are <u>fresh</u> (and) <u>sweet</u>.
   (a.) adjective   d. adverb
   b. noun   e. gerund
   c. verb   f. infinitive

2. These apples and pears are fresh.
   a. adjective   d. adverb
   b. noun   e. gerund
   c. verb   f. infinitive

3. I washed and dried the apples.
   a. adjective   d. adverb
   b. noun   e. gerund
   c. verb   f. infinitive

4. I am washing and drying the apples.
   a. adjective   d. adverb
   b. noun   e. gerund
   c. verb   f. infinitive

5. We ate the fruit happily and quickly.
   a. adjective   d. adverb
   b. noun   e. gerund
   c. verb   f. infinitive

6. Those organic apples are delicious but expensive.
   a. adjective   d. adverb
   b. noun   e. gerund
   c. verb   f. infinitive

7. Apples, pears, and bananas are kinds of fruit.
   a. adjective   d. adverb
   b. noun   e. gerund
   c. verb   f. infinitive

8. I like an apple or a banana with my cereal.
   a. adjective   d. adverb
   b. noun   e. gerund
   c. verb   f. infinitive

9. Those apples are red, ripe, and juicy.
   a. adjective   d. adverb
   b. noun   e. gerund
   c. verb   f. infinitive

PRACTICE 4 ▶ Parallel structure. (Chart 16-1)

Complete each conversation with the correct word or phrase from the list. Write the letter.

a. carefully	e. reliable health care
b. excellence in	f. responsible
c. in agriculture	g. seeking practical solutions
d. provide quality education	h. finds a way to get the important jobs done

1. Mr. Li has had a wide range of experience. He has worked in business, in the news media, and _____.

2. People want safe homes, good schools, and _____.

3. As a taxpayer, I want my money used wisely and _____.

4. Ms. Adams is respected for researching issues and _____.

5. Ms. Hunter has established a record of effective and _____ leadership in government.

6. She has worked hard to control excess government spending, protect our environment, and _____.

7. Carol is a hard-working personnel manager who welcomes challenges and _____.

8. I will continue to fight for adequate funding of and _____ education.

PRACTICE 5 ▶ Parallel structure: using commas. (Chart 16-2)

Add commas as necessary.

1. Jack was calm and quiet.

2. Jack was calm quiet and serene.

3. The soccer players practiced kicking and passing the ball and they ran laps.

4. The soccer players practiced kicking passing and running.

5. The kids collected rocks and insects had a picnic and flew kites.

6. The teacher told the students to put their phones away open their reading books and review their notes.

7. The teacher told the students to put their phones away and open their reading books.

8. Did you know that the pupil of your eye expands and contracts slightly with each heartbeat?

pupil

9. Our server carried two cups of coffee three glasses of water one glass of orange juice and three orders of eggs on her tray.

10. My parents were strict but fair with their children.

PRACTICE 6 ▶ Parallel structure. (Charts 16-1 and 16-2)

Underline the words that are supposed to be parallel. Write "C" if the parallel structure is correct. Write "I" if the parallel structure is incorrect, and make any necessary corrections.

1. __I__ I admire my brother for his intelligence, cheerful disposition, and ~~he is honest~~. *honesty*

2. __C__ Abraham Lincoln was a lawyer and a politician.

3. _____ The boat sailed across the lake smoothly and quiet.

4. _____ Barbara studies each problem carefully and works out a solution.

5. _____ Aluminum is plentiful and relatively inexpensive.

6. _____ Many visitors to Los Angeles enjoy visiting Disneyland and to tour movie studios.

7. _____ Children are usually interested in but a little frightened by snakes.

8. _____ So far this term, the students in the writing class have learned how to write thesis statements, organize their material, and summarizing their conclusions.

9. _____ When I looked more closely, I saw that it was not coffee but chocolate on my necktie.

10. _____ Physics explains why water freezes and how the sun produces heat.

11. _____ All plants need light, a suitable climate, and they require an ample supply of water and minerals from the soil.

12. _____ With their keen sight, fine hearing, and refined sense of smell, wolves hunt day or night in quest of elk, deer, moose, or caribou.

PRACTICE 7 ▶ Separating independent clauses with periods; connecting them with *and* and *but*. (Chart 16-3)

Punctuate the sentences by adding commas or periods. Do not add any words. Add capitalization as necessary.

1. The rain stopped the winds died down.

2. The rain stopped and the winds died down.

3. The rain stopped the winds died down and the clouds disappeared.

4. A young boy ran out on the street his mother ran after him.

5. A young boy ran out on the street and his mother ran after him.

6. A young boy ran out on the street his mother ran after him and caught him by his shirt collar.

7. The café serves delicious pastries and coffee and it is always crowded.

8. The café serves delicious pastries and coffee it is always crowded.

9. The café serves delicious pastries, coffee, and ice cream but it is never crowded.

PRACTICE 8 ▶ Connecting independent clauses with *and* and *but*. (Chart 16-3)

Combine each pair of sentences with the conjunction in parentheses.

1. (*and*) Sherri's graduation was last week. Now she's looking for a job.

   _____

2. (*and*) She completed her degree in nursing. She also has a certificate in radiology.

   _____

3. *(but)* Sherri doesn't have any full-time work experience. She completed a one-year internship at the hospital.

_____

4. *(but)* There is a job opening at Lakeside Hospital. It requires five years of nursing experience.

_____

PRACTICE 9 ▶ Separating independent clauses with periods; connecting them with *and* and *but*. (Chart 16-3)

Correct the errors in punctuation and capitalization.

1. My brother is visiting me for a couple of days we spent yesterday together in the city and we had a really good time.

2. first I took him to the waterfront we went to the aquarium we saw fearsome sharks some wonderfully funny marine mammals and all kinds of tropical fish after the aquarium, we went downtown to the mall and went shopping.

3. I had trouble thinking of a place to take him for lunch because he's a strict vegetarian but I remembered a restaurant that has vegan food we went there and we had a wonderful lunch of fresh vegetables and whole grains I'm not a vegetarian but I must say that I really enjoyed the meal.

4. In the afternoon it started raining we decided to go to a movie it was pretty good but had too much violence for me I felt tense when we left the theater I prefer comedies or dramas my brother loved the movie.

5. We ended the day with a delicious home-cooked meal and some good conversation in my living room it was an excellent day I like spending time with my brother.

PRACTICE 10 ▶ Paired conjunctions: *both ... and; not only ... but also; either ... or; neither ... nor*. (Chart 16-4)

Complete the sentences with the correct present tense form of the verbs in parentheses.

1. Neither the students nor the teacher *(know)* _____*knows*_____ the answer.

2. Neither the teacher nor the students *(know)* _____*know*_____ the answer.

3. Not only the students but also the teacher *(know)* _____ the answer.

4. Not only the teacher but also the students *(know)* _____ the answer.

5. Both the teacher and the students *(know)* _____ the answer.

6. Neither Alan nor Carol *(want)* _____ to go skiing this weekend.

7. Both John and Ted *(like)* _____ to go cross-country skiing.

8. Either Jack or Alice *(have)* _____ the information you need.

9. Neither my parents nor my brother *(agree)* _____ with my decision.

10. Both intelligence and skill *(be)* _____ essential to good teaching.

11. Neither my classmates nor my teacher *(realize)* _____ that I have no idea what's going on in class.

12. Not only my husband but also my children *(be)* _____ in favor of my decision to return to school and finish my graduate degree.

PRACTICE 11 ▶ Paired conjunctions: *both ... and; not only ... but also; either ... or; neither ... nor.* (Chart 16-4)

Write sentences with the given words and the paired conjunctions. Use capital letters and punctuation as necessary.

1. Mary drinks coffee. Her parents drink coffee.

    a. both ... and _____ .

    b. neither ... nor _____ .

2. John will do the work. Henry will do the work.

    a. either ... or _____ .

    b. neither ... nor _____ .

3. Our school recycles trash. Our school recycles old electronics.

    a. not only ... but also _____ .

    b. both ... and _____ .

PRACTICE 12 ▶ Paired conjunctions: *both ... and; not only ... but also; either ... or; neither ... nor.* (Chart 16-4)

Complete the sentences.

Part I. Use *both ... and*.

1. You know her mother. Do you know her father too?

    Yes, _____*I know both her mother and her father.*_____

2. The nurses usually arrive early. Does the doctor arrive early too?

    Yes, _____ early.

3. Bananas originated in Asia. Did mangos originate in Asia too?

    Yes, _____ in Asia.

4. Whales are mammals. Are dolphins mammals too?

    Yes, _____ mammals.

Part II. Use *not only ... but also*.

5. Ethiopia exports coffee. Does it export oil too?

    Ethiopia _____ .

6. Air Greenland flies to Greenland. What about Icelandair?

    _____ to Greenland.

7. You bought a lime-green jacket. What about pants? Did you buy lime-green pants too?

    Yes, I bought _____ to go with it.

8. Al attended Harvard University. Did he attend Harvard Law School too?

    Yes, Al _____ .

Part III. Use *either ... or*.

9. Someone knows the answer. Is it Ricky? Paula? One of them knows.

   _____ the answer.

10. You're going to Mexico on your vacation. Are you going to Costa Rica too?

    We're going _____, not

    to both.

11. Who will take Taka to the airport: Jim or Taka's parents?

    _____ to the airport.

12. Helen's buying salmon. Is she buying tuna too?

    No. She's buying _____,

    whichever looks fresher.

Part IV. Use *neither ... nor*.

13. Fred doesn't eat red meat. Do his children eat red meat?

    No, _____ eat red meat.

14. She doesn't have health insurance. Do her children have health insurance?

    No, _____ health insurance.

15. Luis doesn't have a family. Does he have friends?

    No, _____.

16. How's the weather there? Is it hot? Is it cold?

    It's perfect! It's _____.

PRACTICE 13 ▶ Chapter review.
Correct the errors. Add the necessary punctuation.

1. Either John will call Mary or Bob.

2. Not only Sue saw the mouse but also the cat.

3. Both my mother talked to the teacher and my father.

4. Either Mr. Anderson or Ms. Wiggins are going to teach our class today.

5. I enjoy not only reading novels but also magazines I enjoy.

6. Smallpox is a dangerous disease. Malaria too. Both are dangerous.

7. She wants to buy a compact car, she is saving her money.

8. According to the news report, it will snow tonight the roads may be dangerous in the morning.

9. While we were in New York, we attended an opera, while we were in New York, we ate at marvelous restaurants, we visited some old friends.

Complete the crossword puzzle. Use the clues under the puzzle. All the words come from Chapter 16.

Across

3. I drink tea, _____ I don't drink coffee.

4. Carl is not _____ a chemist but also a biologist.

6. Thankfully, _____ Mary or Joe will help us.

7. He has neither friends _____ money.

Down

1. _____ Jane nor Al speaks Spanish.

2. _____ Sue and Sam are doctors.

5. Salt _____ pepper are on the table.

CHAPTER 17

Adverb Clauses

PRACTICE 1 ▸ Preview.
Read the passage. Answer the questions.

Staying Connected

Before social media sites existed, it was often difficult to stay connected with friends and family or find old friends. Now that we have access to a multitude of social media sites, it's easy to be in touch with people. While most people agree that this is true, some are worried that social media does exactly the opposite. Even though we can stay in touch with a large number of people through social media, those connections are not always very deep. As more and more people rely on social media for communication, they are spending less time having real conversations. Whenever we have an important announcement to make to our friends, we might write a couple of sentences on a social media site for everyone to see because it is more efficient than making several phone calls. In some extreme cases, people report communicating with their friends mostly through social media sites even if they live in the same house as those friends. Whether or not we like it, social media sites are probably here to stay. They can be beneficial as long as we remember that it's also important to connect with our friends individually through phone calls or face-to-face meetings.

---

1. Which words express a time relationship?

   _____

2. Which words express a cause-and-effect relationship?

   _____

3. Which words express contrast?

   _____

4. Which words express condition?

   _____

PRACTICE 2 ▸ Adverb clauses. (Chart 17-1)
<u>Underline</u> the adverb clause in each sentence.

1. Sanae dropped a carton of eggs as she was leaving the store.

2. Tomorrow, we'll all go for a run in the park before we have breakfast.

3. Since Douglas fell off his bike last week, he has had to use crutches to walk.

4. Because I already had my boarding pass, I didn't have to stand in line at the airline counter.

5. Productivity in a factory increases if the workplace is made pleasant.

6. After Ceylon had been independent for 24 years, its name was changed to Sri Lanka.

7. Ms. Johnson regularly answers her email messages as soon as she receives them.

8. Tarik will be able to work more efficiently once he becomes familiar with the new computer program.

PRACTICE 3 ▸ Periods and commas. (Chart 17-1)
Add periods and commas as necessary. Do not change, add, or omit any words. Capitalize as necessary.

1. The lake was calm Tom went fishing.

2. Because the lake was calm Tom went fishing.

3. Tom went fishing because the lake was calm he caught two fish.

4. When Tom went fishing the lake was calm he caught two fish.

5. The lake was calm so Tom went fishing he caught two fish.

6. Because the lake was calm and quiet Tom went fishing.

7. The lake was calm quiet and clear when Tom went fishing.

8. Because Mr. Hood has dedicated his life to helping the poor he is admired in his community.

9. Mr. Hood is admired because he has dedicated his life to helping the poor he is well known for his work on behalf of homeless people.

10. Microscopes automobile dashboards and cameras are awkward for left-handed people to use they are designed for right-handed people when "lefties" use these items they have to use their right hand to do the things that they would normally do with their left hand.

PRACTICE 4 ▸ Using adverb clauses to show time relationships. (Charts 17-1 and 17-2)
Choose the correct completions.

1. After Ismael _____ his degree, he plans to seek employment in an engineering firm.
   a. will finish   b. finishes   c. is going to finish   d. is finishing

2. By the time Colette leaves work today, she _____ the budget report.
   a. will finish   b. finishes   c. will have finished   d. had finished

3. When my aunt _____ at the airport tomorrow, I'll be at work, so I can't pick her up.
   a. will arrive   b. arrived   c. will have arrived   d. arrives

4. Natasha heard a small "meow" and looked down to discover a kitten at her feet. When she saw it, she _____.
   a. is smiling   b. had smiled   c. smiled   d. smiles

5. Ahmed has trouble keeping a job. By the time Ahmed was 30, he _____ eight different jobs.
   a. has   b. was having   c. had had   d. had been having

6. Maria waits until her husband, Allen, _____ to work before she calls her friends on the phone.
   a. will go   b. went   c. will have gone   d. goes

7. I went to an opera at Lincoln Center the last time I _____ to New York City.
   a. go   b. went   c. had gone   d. have gone

8. When the police arrived, the building was empty. The thieves _____ and escaped through an unlocked window.
   a. will have   b. have entered   c. had entered   d. were entering

9. It seems that whenever I try to take some quiet time for myself, the phone _____.
   a. has been ringing   b. rings   c. is ringing   d. has rung

10. I'll invite the Thompsons to the potluck dinner the next time I _____ them.
    a. see   b. will see   c. will have seen   d. have seen

11. I _____ hard to help support my family ever since I was a child.
    a. worked   b. work   c. am working   d. have worked

12. A small rabbit ran across the path in front of me as I _____ through the woods.
    a. was walking   b. had walked   c. am walking   d. had been walking

PRACTICE 5 ▸ Using adverb clauses to show time relationships. (Chart 17-2)
Write "1" before the event that happened first. Write "2" before the event that happened second.
Write "S" for *same* if the events happened at the same time.

1. As soon as it stopped snowing, the kids ran out to go sledding in the fresh snow.

   __1__ It stopped snowing.

   __2__ The kids ran out to go sledding.

2. I'll call you as soon as we arrive at the motel.

   _____ I'll call you.

   _____ We arrive at the hotel.

3. We turned on the heat when it got cold.

   _____ It got cold.

   _____ We turned on the heat.

4. We will turn on the heat when it gets cold.

   _____ We will turn on the heat.

   _____ It will get cold.

5. By the time Sharon gets home from Africa, she will have been away for two years.

   _____ Sharon gets home.

   _____ She will have been away.

6. By the time Marc graduated from medical school, he had been studying for 20 years.

   _____ He had been studying.

   _____ Marc graduated from medical school.

7. We were crying while we were watching the movie.

   _____ We were crying.

   _____ We were watching the movie.

8. When I have some news, I'll tell you.

   _____ I have some news.

   _____ I'll tell you.

PRACTICE 6 ▸ Using adverb clauses to show cause and effect. (Chart 17-3)

Complete the sentences in Column A with a clause from Column B.

Column A

1. I left a message on Jane's voicemail because _____.
2. Since everybody in my office dresses informally, _____.
3. Now that it's summer, _____.
4. Our carpool was late because _____.
5. Because the temperature dropped below 0 degrees C (32 degrees F), _____.
6. Olivia hopes to find a good job now that _____.
7. I'm not going to the party since _____.
8. We had to eat dinner by candlelight because _____.
9. Since their favorite restaurant was closed, _____.
10. I prefer a small car because _____.

Column B

a. the days are longer
b. they went to another one
c. I wasn't invited
d. she didn't answer her phone
e. there was a big traffic jam
f. the power went out
g. it uses less gasoline
h. the water in the lake froze
i. I usually wear jeans to work
j. she has received her master's degree in business

PRACTICE 7 ▸ Using adverb clauses to show cause and effect. (Chart 17-3)

Combine the sentences. Write one clause in each blank.

1. My registration was canceled. I didn't pay the registration fee on time.

   _____ because _____.

2. I'm late. There was a lot of traffic.

   _____ because _____.

3. Harry lost 35 pounds. He was on a strict weight-loss diet.

   Because _____, _____.

4. We can't have lunch at Mario's tomorrow. It is closed on Sundays.

   Since _____, _____.

5. Jack drives to work. He has a car.

   Now that _____, _____.

6. Natalie should find another job. She is very unhappy in this job.

   _____ since _____.

7. David knows the way. He will lead us.

   _____ because _____.

8. Frank has graduated from law school. He is looking for a job in a law office.

   _____ now that _____.

PRACTICE 8 ▸ *Even though* vs. *because*. (Chart 17-4)

Choose the correct completions.

1. I put on my raincoat   even though / because   it was a bright, sunny day.
2. I put on my raincoat   even though / because   it was raining.
3. Even though / Because   Sue is a good student, she received a scholarship.
4. Even though / Because   Ann is a good student, she didn't receive a scholarship.
5. Even though / Because   I was so tired, I didn't want to walk all the way home. I took a taxi.
6. Even though / Because   I was dead tired, I walked all the way home.
7. This letter was delivered   even though / because   it didn't have enough postage.
8. That letter was returned to the sender   even though / because   it didn't have enough postage.

PRACTICE 9 ▸ *Even though* vs. *because*. (Chart 17-4)

Complete the sentences with *even though* or *because*.

1. a. I'm going horseback riding with Judy this afternoon _____ I'm afraid of horses.

   b. I'm going horseback riding with Judy this afternoon _____ I enjoy it.

2. a. _____ the economy is not good right now, people are not buying new cars and other expensive items.

   b. _____ the economy is not good right now, the supermarket is still a profitable business. People always have to eat.

3. a. Members of the Polar Bear Club are swimmers who go swimming in the ocean _____ the temperature may be freezing.

   b. Members of the Polar Bear Club are swimmers who swim in the ocean every day in summer and winter _____ they love to swim in the ocean.

4. a. Janet got a grade of 98% on her history test _____ she studied hard.

   b. Mike got a grade of 98% on his history test _____ he didn't study at all. I wonder how that happened.

PRACTICE 10 ▸ Showing direct contrast: *while*. (Chart 17-5)

Choose the phrase that shows direct contrast.

1. Larry and Barry are twins, but they are very different. Larry never studies, while Barry _____.
   a. rarely studies
   b. sleeps all day
   c. is very studious

2. My roommate and I disagree about the room temperature. While she likes it warm, I _____.
   a. prefer cold temperatures
   b. have trouble when it is cool
   c. don't like my roommate

3. Athletes need to be strong, but they may need different physical characteristics for different sports.

For example, weight-lifters have well-developed chest muscles, while _____.
a. basketball players' muscles are strong
b. basketball players should be tall
c. basketball players' chest muscles are very large

4. Portland, Maine, is on the East Coast of the United States, while Portland, Oregon, _____.
a. is on the East Coast too
b. lies on the West Coast
c. is another medium-sized city

5. Crocodiles and alligators look a lot alike, but they have certain differences.

While a crocodile has a very long, narrow, V-shaped snout, the alligator's snout is _____.
a. wider and U-shaped
b. long, narrow, and V-shaped
c. large and green

6. The Earth is similar to Venus in some ways, but their atmospheres are different. While the Earth's atmosphere contains mostly nitrogen and oxygen, _____.
a. Venus has mainly nitrogen and oxygen
b. Venus' air is very cold
c. Venus' atmosphere consists mostly of the gas carbon dioxide

7. Polar bears live near the North Pole, while _____.
a. penguins live there too
b. penguins live at the South Pole
c. they live in the South Pole

8. Potatoes and tomatoes originated in the Americas, while _____.
a. mangos and bananas come from Asia
b. corn and chocolate come from the Americas
c. turkeys first lived in North America

PRACTICE 11 ▸ *If*-clauses. (Chart 17-6)

Underline the entire *if*-clause. Correct any errors in verb forms. Some sentences have no errors.

1. We won't go to the beach if it ~~will rain~~ *rains* tomorrow.

2. If my car doesn't start tomorrow morning, I'll take the bus to work.

3. If I have any free time during my workday, I'll call you.

4. I'll text you if my phone won't die.

5. If we don't leave within the next ten minutes, we are late for the theater.

6. If we will leave within the next ten minutes, we will make it to the theater on time.

7. The population of the world will be 9.1 billion in 2050 if it will continue to grow at the present rate.

PRACTICE 12 ▸ Shortened *if*-clauses. (Chart 17-7)

First, complete the sentences in two ways:

    a. Use ***so*** or ***not***.

    b. Use a helping verb or main verb ***be***.

Second, give the full meaning of the shortened ***if-clause***.

1. Does Asraf live near you?

    a. If _____*so*_____, ask him to pick you up at 5:30.

    b. If he _____*does*_____, ask him to pick you up at 5:30.

    Meaning: _____*If Asraf lives near you*_____

2. Are you a resident of Springfield?

    a. If _____, you can get a library card for the Springfield Library.

    b. If you _____, you can get a library card for the Springfield Library.

    Meaning: _____

3. Do you have enough money to go out to dinner?

    a. If _____, I'll pay for you.

    b. If you _____, I'll pay for you.

    Meaning: _____

4. Are you going to do the laundry?

    a. If _____, I have some things that need washing too.

    b. If you _____, I have some things that need washing too.

    Meaning: _____

5. I think I left the water running in the sink.

    a. If _____, we'd better go home and turn it off.

    b. If I _____, we'd better go home and turn it off.

    Meaning: _____

PRACTICE 13 ▸ Using *whether or not* and *even if*. (Chart 17-8)

Complete the sentences using the given information.

1. Juan is going to major in photography no matter what. He doesn't care if his parents approve. In other words, Juan is going to major in photography even if his parents _____*don't approve*_____.
He's going to get a degree in photography whether his parents _____*approve*_____ or not.

2. Fatima is determined to buy an expensive car. It doesn't matter to her if she can't afford it. In other words, Fatima is going to buy an expensive car whether she _____ it or not. She's going to buy one even if she _____ it.

3. William wears his raincoat every day. He wears it when it's raining. He wears it when it's not raining. In other words, William wears his raincoat whether it _____ or not. He wears it even if it _____.

4. Some students don't understand what the teacher is saying, but still they smile and nod. In other words, even if they _____ what the teacher is saying, they smile and nod. They smile and nod whether they _____ what the teacher is saying or not.

5. Everybody has to pay taxes. It doesn't matter whether you want to or not. In other words, even if you _____, you have to pay them. You have to pay your taxes _____ or not.

PRACTICE 14 ▸ Adverb clause of condition: using *in case*. (17-9)
Complete the sentences in Column A with a clause from Column B.

Column A

1. You should take a jacket _____.

2. Be sure to save your work _____.

3. I brought a charger _____.

4. Here's my number _____.

5. I picked up some local travel brochures _____.

6. Dr. Kennedy is on call tonight _____.

7. I put the salad dressing on the side _____.

8. Take your car to the mechanic before you leave for your trip _____.

Column B

a. in case my phone dies.

b. in case you need to reach me

c. in case you're interested in taking a day trip

d. in case a patient has a medical emergency

e. in case it gets cold tonight

f. just in case your computer crashes

g. just in case it has any problems

h. in case you don't like it

PRACTICE 15 ▸ Adverb clauses of condition: using *unless*. (Chart 17-10)
The sentences in *italics* are well-known proverbs or sayings. Write sentences with the same meaning as the sentences in *italics*. Use **unless**.

1. *If you can't stand the heat, get out of the kitchen.*

   This means that if you can't take the pressure, then you should remove yourself from the situation.

   Get out of the kitchen unless you can stand the heat _____.

2. *If it isn't broken, don't fix it.* This is often said as *If it ain't broke, don't fix it.*

   This means that any attempt to improve something that already works is pointless and may even hurt it.

   Don't fix it _____.

3. *If you can't beat them, join them.*

   This means if you can't beat your opponents, you can join them.

   You might not be successful _____.

4. *If you scratch my back, I'll scratch yours.*

   This means that if you help me, I'll help you too.

   I might not help you _____.

5. *If you're in a hole, stop digging.*

   This means that you should try not to make a problem worse than it already is.

   A hole will continue to get bigger _____.

PRACTICE 16 ▸ Adverb clauses of condition: using *only if*. (Chart 17-11)
Complete the sentences with the information in the given sentence.

1. Jason never calls his uncle unless he wants something.

   Jason calls his uncle only if _____ .

2. When Helen runs out of clean clothes, she does her laundry. Otherwise, she never does laundry.

   Helen does laundry only if _____ .

3. José doesn't like to turn on the heat in his house unless the temperature outside goes below
   50 degrees F (10 degrees C).

   José turns on the heat only if _____ .

4. Zach hates to fly. He usually travels by car or train except when it is absolutely necessary to get
   somewhere quickly.

   Zach flies only if _____ .

5. Most applicants cannot get into Halley College. You probably won't get in. Only the top students
   will get in.

   Only if you are a top student _____ .

6. I could never afford a big house like that! Well, maybe if I win the lottery. That would be the only way.

   Only if I win the lottery _____ .

PRACTICE 17 ▸ Review: adverb clauses of condition. (Charts 17-8 → 17-11)
Choose the word to logically complete each sentence.

1. I'll pass the course only if I   pass / don't pass   the final examination.
2. I'm   going to go / not going to go   to the park unless the weather is nice.
3. I'm going to the park unless it   rains / doesn't rain.
4. I'm sorry that you won't be able to join us on Saturday. But please call us   in case / even if   you
   change your mind.
5. Roberto doesn't like to work. He'll get a job   unless / only if   he has to.
6. I   always eat / never eat   breakfast unless I get up late and don't have enough time.
7. I always finish my homework   even if / only if   I'm sleepy and want to go to bed.
8. Ali is at his desk at 8:00 A.M. sharp   whether / unless   his boss is there or not.
9. You   will / won't   learn to play the guitar well unless you practice every day.
10. Even if the president calls,   wake / don't wake   me up. I don't want to talk to anyone.
    I need to sleep.
11. Burt is going to come to the game with us today   if / unless   his boss gives him the afternoon off.
12. Only if people succeed in reducing greenhouse gases   we can / can we   avoid the effects
    of global warming.

PRACTICE 18 ▶ Chapter review.

Complete each conversation with the correct phrase from the list. Write the letter.

a. her friend goes with her
b. I don't eat meat
c. I don't have an 8:00 A.M. class anymore
d. I eat meat
e. I work weekends now
f. none of her friends will go with her
g. you have a real emergency
h. you promise to keep it a secret

1. A: Won't you tell me about Emma and Tom? Oh, please tell me!

   B: Well, OK, I'll tell you, but only if _____.

2. A: Hello, 911? Police? I want to report a barking dog.

   B: This is 911. You've dialed the wrong number. Call this number only in case _____.

3. A: Isn't Sara coming to the party?

   B: I don't think so. She's too shy to come alone. She doesn't go anyplace unless _____.

4. A: Your grandmother has traveled to 32 countries all by herself?

   B: Yes, she has! She loves to travel to exotic places even if _____.

5. A: Do you want to go to Johnson's Steak House or Vernon's Vegetable Stand for lunch?

   B: Definitely Vernon's Vegetable Stand since _____.

6. A: They say that people who don't eat meat live longer than people who do.

   B: Well, I think that I will live a certain number of years whether or not _____.

7. A: You haven't come to our book club for months! How come?

   B: Oh, I can't come on Saturdays anymore because _____.

8. A: Hi, Kevin. ... Oh, did I wake you up? It's 7:30 already! You need to get up.

   B: I sleep later now, Andy, since _____.

PRACTICE 19 ▶ Chapter review.

Choose the correct completions.

1. Alice will tutor you in math _____ you promise to show up promptly every day.
   a. unless   b. only if   c. whereas   d. even though

2. Oscar won't pass his math course _____ he gets a tutor.
   a. in case   b. unless   c. only if   d. because

3. Most people you meet will be polite to you _____ you are polite to them.
   a. in case   b. even though   c. unless   d. if

4. I'm glad that my mother made me take piano lessons when I was a child _____ I hated it at the time.
   Now, I enjoy playing the piano every day.
   a. even though   b. because   c. unless   d. if

5. Chicken eggs will not hatch _____ they are kept at the proper temperature.
   a. because   b. unless   c. only if   d. even though

6. You'd better take your raincoat with you _____ the weather changes. It could rain before you get home again.
   a. now that   b. even if   c. in case   d. only if

7. Vanessa got the research fellowship _____ she had the best qualifications of all the applicants.
   a. although   b. whereas   c. if   d. since

8. My sister can fall asleep under any conditions, but I can't get to sleep _____ the light is off and the room is perfectly quiet.

a. if   b. unless   c. in case   d. now that

9. In a democratic government, a leader is directly responsible to the people, _____ in a dictatorship, a leader has no direct responsibility to the people.

a. because   b. even though   c. while   d. unless

10. Parents love and support their children _____ the children misbehave or do foolish things.

a. even if   b. since   c. if   d. only if

Reduction of Adverb Clauses to Modifying Adverbial Phrases

PRACTICE 1 ▸ Preview.
Underline the ten adverb clause or phrases.

> **Coloring Books for Adults**
>
> Coloring books for children have always been popular, but lately many adults have been buying coloring books for themselves. These days, it's not unusual to see an adult coloring pages while waiting for a doctor's appointment or sitting on a bus. Looking for an easy activity to relieve stress, some people turn to coloring. Research has shown that anxiety levels drop when people color. Coloring is similar to meditation because it helps people focus on the moment while allowing the brain to switch off other thoughts or worries. Other people enjoy coloring because they feel that they can be creative even if they don't have the artistic ability to draw something from scratch. Still others are looking for an escape from technology. Constantly staring at screens all day, adults need a chance to "unplug." Nostalgia is yet another reason for the sudden popularity of adult coloring books. Wanting to feel like a kid again, an adult might open up a coloring book. Since becoming a trend, adult coloring books have become widely available. They can be found in almost any bookstore and have even been included on bestseller lists.

PRACTICE 2 ▸ Modifying adverbial phrases. (Chart 18-2)
Check (✓) the grammatically correct sentences.

1. _____ While watching an exciting program, the TV suddenly went off.

2. _____ While starting up, my computer suddenly crashed.

3. _____ While listening to a podcast, I fell asleep.

4. _____ Before going to bed, I always open the bedroom windows.

5. _____ Before going to bed, the bedroom windows are always open.

6. _____ After opening the bedroom windows, I crawl into bed for the night.

7. _____ Since graduating from college, nobody has offered me a job.

8. _____ Since graduating from college, I haven't found a job.

9. _____ After sitting on her eggs for four weeks, we saw the mother duck welcome her baby ducklings.

10. _____ After sitting on her eggs for four weeks, the mother duck welcomed her baby ducklings.

PRACTICE 3 ▸ Changing time clauses to modifying adverbial phrases. (Chart 18-2)
Change the adverb clause to a modifying phrase.

1. Since ~~he opened~~ *opening* his new business, Liam has been working 16 hours a day.

2. I shut off the lights before I left the room.

3. After I had met the movie star in person, I understood why she was so popular.

4. After I searched through all my pockets, I found my keys.

5. While he was herding his goats in the mountains, an Ethiopian named Kaldi discovered the coffee plant more than 1,200 years ago.

6. Before they marched into battle, ancient Ethiopian soldiers ate a mixture of coffee beans and fat for extra energy.

7. While she was flying across the Pacific Ocean in 1937, the famous pilot Amelia Earhart disappeared.

8. After they imported rabbits to Australia, the settlers found that these animals became pests.

PRACTICE 4 ▸ Adverb clauses and modifying phrases. (Charts 18-1 → 18-3)
Complete the sentences with the correct form of the verbs in parentheses.

1. a. Before (*leave*) ___*leaving*___ on his trip, Tom renewed his passport.

   b. Before Tom (*leave*) ___*left*___ on his trip, he renewed his passport.

2. a. After Thomas Edison (*invent*) ___*invented / had invented*___ the light bulb, he went on to create many other useful inventions.

   b. After (*invent*) ___*inventing / having invented*___ the light bulb, Thomas Edison went on to create many other useful inventions.

3. a. While (*work*) _____ with uranium ore, Marie Curie discovered two new elements, radium and polonium.

   b. While she (*work*) _____ with uranium ore, Marie Curie discovered two new elements, radium and polonium.

4. a. Before an astronaut (*fly*) _____ on a space mission, she will have undergone thousands of hours of training.

   b. Before (*fly*) _____ on a space mission, an astronaut will have undergone thousands of hours of training.

5. a. After they (*study*) _____ the stars, the ancient Maya in Central America developed a very accurate solar calendar.

   b. After (*study*) _____ the stars, the ancient Maya in Central America developed a very accurate solar calendar.

6. a. Since (*learn*) _____ that cigarettes cause cancer, the medical profession has encouraged people to quit smoking.

   b. Since they (*learn*) _____ that cigarettes cause cancer, the medical profession has encouraged people to quit smoking.

7. a. When (*take*) _____ any medication, you should be sure to follow the

   directions on the label.

   b. When you (*take*) _____ any medication, you should be sure to follow the

   directions on the label.

8. a. While I (*drive*) _____ to my uncle's house, I took a wrong turn and

   ended up back where I had started.

   b. While (*drive*) _____ to my uncle's house, I took a wrong turn and ended

   up back where I had started.

PRACTICE 5 ▸ Adverb clauses and modifying phrases. (Charts 18-1 → 18-3)

Underline the subject of the adverb clause and the subject of the main clause. Change the adverb clauses to modifying phrases if possible.

1. While Sam was driving to work in the rain, his car got a flat tire.

   _____ (no change) _____

2. While Sam was driving to work, he had a flat tire.

   _____ While driving to work, Sam had a flat tire. _____

3. Before Nick left on his trip, his son gave him a big hug and a kiss.

   _____

4. Before Nick left on his trip, he gave his itinerary to his secretary.

   _____

5. After Tom had worked hard in the garden all afternoon, he took a shower and then went to the movies with his friends.

   _____

6. After Sunita had made a delicious chicken curry for her friends, they wanted the recipe.

   _____

7. Emily always clears off her desk before she leaves the office at the end of each day.

   _____

PRACTICE 6 ▸ Expressing the idea of "during the same time" and cause/effect in modifying adverbial clauses. (Charts 18-3 and 18-4)

Underline the modifying adverbial phrase in each sentence. Then choose the meaning of each modifying phrase. In some sentences, both meanings may be given.

1. Riding his bicycle to school, Enrique fell off and scraped his knee.
   a. while   b. because

2. Being seven feet tall, the basketball player couldn't sit in a regular airplane seat.
   a. while   b. because

3. Driving to work this morning, I remembered that I had already missed the special 8:00 A.M. breakfast meeting.
   a. while   b. because

4. Running five miles on a very hot day, James felt exhausted.
   a. while   b. because

5. Having run for 26 miles in the marathon, the runners were exhausted at the end of the race.
   a. while   b. because

6. Drinking a tall glass of refreshing iced tea, Ann felt her tired muscles relax.
   a. while   b. because

7. Clapping loudly at the end of the game, the fans showed their appreciation of the team.
   a. while   b. because

8. Speaking with her guidance counselor, Clara felt that she was being understood.
   a. while   b. because

9. Knowing that I was going to miss the plane because of heavy traffic, I contacted the airline about taking a later flight.
   a. while   b. because

10. Having missed my plane, I had to wait four hours to take the next one.
    a. while   b. because

11. Waiting for my plane to depart, I watched thousands of people walking through the airport.
    a. while   b. because

PRACTICE 7 ▸ Expressing the idea of "during the same time" and cause/effect in modifying adverbial phrases. (Charts 18-3 and 18-4)

Complete the sentences in Column A with a clause from Column B.

Column A

1. Rushing to the airport, _____ .

2. While watching an old movie on TV _____ .

3. Drinking a big glass of water in four seconds, _____ .

4. Because I like old movies, _____ .

5. Since receiving a big job promotion, _____ .

6. Having finished my long report, _____ .

7. Unable to reach my friend by phone, _____ .

8. Being a shy person, _____ .

9. Having lived in Rome for two years, _____ .

10. Wanting to get home quickly, _____ .

Column B

a. I handed it in to my supervisor this morning

b. I watch a lot of them on TV late at night

c. I decided to email her

d. I have more responsibility

e. I can speak Italian

f. I don't like to go to parties alone

g. I ran all the way

h. I forgot my passport at home

i. I fell asleep

j. I quenched my thirst

PRACTICE 8 ▸ Modifying phrases and clauses. (Charts 18-2 → 18-4)

Choose all the possible completions for each sentence. More than one answer may be possible.

1. Before _____ you, I had not known such a wonderful person existed!
   a. met   b. meeting   c. I met

2. After _____ what the candidate had to say, I am considering voting for him.
   a. I heard   b. having heard   c. hearing

3. Since _____ married, Fred seems very happy and content.
   a. he got   b. getting   c. got

4. _____ through outer space at a speed of 25,000 miles per hour (40,000 kilometers), the astronauts were able to see the Earth.
   a. Speeding   b. While speeding   c. Sped

5. _____ president of his new country, George Washington had been a general in its army.
    a. Before becoming   b. While becoming   c. Before he became

6. _____ rap music before, our grandparents wondered why it was so popular.
    a. Had never heard   b. Because they had never heard   c. Never having heard

7. _____ the English faculty, Professor Wilson has become the most popular teacher at our university.
    a. Since joining   b. While joining   c. Since he joined

PRACTICE 9 ▸ Modifying phrases with *upon*. (Chart 18-5)
Rewrite the sentences with the given words.

1. When Sarah received her acceptance letter for medical school, she shouted for joy.

    a. Upon _____ .

    b. On _____ .

2. On hearing the sad news, Kathleen began to cry.

    a. Upon _____ .

    b. When _____ .

3. Upon looking at the accident victim, the paramedics decided to transport him to the hospital.

    a. On _____ .

    b. When _____ .

PRACTICE 10 ▸ Modifying phrases with *upon*. (Chart 18-5)
Complete the sentences using the ideas from the list.

    a. She learned the problem was not at all serious.
    b. She was told she got it.
    c. She discovered a burned-out wire.
    d. She arrived at the airport.
    e. She reached the other side of the lake.

1. It had been a long, uncomfortable trip. Upon _____*arriving at the airport*_____, Sue quickly
    unfastened her seat belt and stood in the aisle waiting her turn to disembark.

2. Kim rented a small fishing boat last weekend, but she ended up doing more rowing than fishing.
    The motor died halfway across the lake, so she had to row to shore. It was a long distance away.
    Upon _____ , she was exhausted.

3. At first, we thought the fire had been caused by lightning. However, upon
    _____ , the fire chief determined it had been
    caused by faulty electrical wiring.

4. Amy felt terrible. She was sure she had some terrible disease, so she went to the doctor for some
    tests. Upon _____ , she was extremely relieved.

5. Vanessa wanted that scholarship with all her heart and soul. Upon
    _____ , she jumped straight up in the air and let
    out a scream of happiness.

PRACTICE 11 ▸ Modifying phrases. (Charts 18-1 → 18-5)
Write the letter of the clause from the list that logically follows the modifying phrase.

    a. the desperate woman grasped a floating log after the boat turned over
    b. the taxi driver caused a multiple-car accident
    c. carefully proofread all your answers
    d. the doctor asked the patient more questions
    e. the athletes waved to the cheering crowd
    f. the student raised her hand
    g. the manager learned of their dissatisfaction with their jobs
    h. the passengers angrily walked back to the ticket counter
    i. Margo hasn't been able to play tennis
    j. Micah requested to meet with the Teaching Assistant.

1. Trying to better understand the problem, _____.

2. Fighting for her life, _____.

3. Wanting to ask her professor a question, _____.

4. After having injured her ankle, _____.

5. Not wanting to bother his professor, _____.

6. Upon hearing the announcement that their plane was delayed, _____.

7. Talking with the employees after work, _____.

8. Attempting to get onto the freeway, _____.

9. Stepping onto the platform to receive their medals, _____.

10. Before turning in your exam paper, _____.

PRACTICE 12 ▸ Chapter review.
The following sentences contain popular expressions. Change the adverb clauses to modifying phrases if possible.

1. Before a friend tries to do something hard, you may say "Break a leg!" to wish him or her good luck.

   _____

2. After you finish something very easy, you can say it was a "piece of cake."

   _____

3. When something is very expensive, you can say it "costs an arm and a leg."

   _____

4. When you do or say something exactly right, you can say you "hit the nail on the head."

   _____

5. While you are working late in the night, you are "burning the midnight oil."

   _____

6. After you wake up in a bad mood, you can say you "woke up on the wrong side of the bed."

   _____

7. Because I lost all my work when my computer crashed, I went "back to square one."

   _____

8. Because our original plans didn't work, we went "back to the drawing board."

   _____

CHAPTER 19

Connectives That Express Cause and Effect, Contrast, and Condition

PRACTICE 1 ▶ Preview.
Underline the ten connecting words. Then answer the questions.

> **Language and Toys**
>
> Parents often buy noisy electronic toys for their babies because these toys seem educational. If a toy talks or plays music, many parents believe that the toy is teaching the sounds and structure of language. However, some researchers believe electronic toys actually delay language development in small children. They believe this happens due to a lack of human interaction. Because of their busy schedules, parents often buy electronic toys to keep their children occupied. Consequently, these parents might spend less time talking to and interacting with their children. While electronic toys are entertaining, the most important skill for babies to learn is how to communicate with other people. Even if electronic toys sing the alphabet or say the names of shapes and colors, they do not promote communication. On the other hand, more traditional toys such as puzzles and blocks seem to encourage babies to communicate. Studies have found that books produce the most communication between parents and babies. Whether or not parents buy electronic toys, they should try to interact with their babies as much as possible.

1. Which connecting words express cause and effect?

   _____

2. Which connecting words express contrast?

   _____

3. Which connecting words express condition?

   _____

PRACTICE 2 ▶ Using *because of* and *due to*. (Chart 19-2)
Choose the correct completions. More than one answer may be correct.

1. The plane was delayed because _____.
   a. bad weather
   b. the weather was bad
   c. there was heavy air traffic
   d. heavy air traffic
   e. mechanical difficulty
   f. the mechanics had to make a repair

2. The plane was delayed because of _____.
   a. bad weather
   b. the weather was bad
   c. there was heavy air traffic
   d. heavy air traffic
   e. mechanical difficulty
   f. the mechanics had to make a repair

3. The burglar was caught because _____.
   a. the police responded quickly
   b. the quick police response
   c. he left fingerprints
   d. the fingerprints on the door
   e. there was a security video
   f. a security video

4. The burglar was caught due to _____.
   a. the police responded quickly
   b. the quick police response
   c. he left fingerprints
   d. the fingerprints on the door
   e. there was a security video
   f. a security video

PRACTICE 3 ▸ Using *because of* and *due to*. (Chart 19-2)
Choose the correct completions. More than one answer may be correct.

1. We delayed our trip   because / because of / due to   Dad was sick with the flu.
2. Claire's eyes were red   due to / because of / because   she had been crying.
3. The water in most rivers is unsafe to drink   because / due to / because of   pollution.
4. The water in most rivers is unsafe to drink   because / due to / because of   it is polluted.
5. Some people think Harry succeeded in business   due to / because of / because   his charming personality rather than his business skills.
6. You can't enter this secured area   because of / because / due to   you don't have proper ID.
7. My lecture notes were incomplete   due to / because of / because   the instructor talked too fast.
8. It's unsafe to travel in that country   because / due to / because of   the ongoing civil war.

PRACTICE 4 ▸ Using *because of* and *due to*. (Chart 19-2)
Use the ideas in parentheses to complete the sentences.

1. (*There was heavy traffic.*) We were late due to _____*heavy trafic*_____.
2. (*There was heavy traffic.*) We were late because _____.
3. (*Grandpa is getting old.*) Grandpa doesn't like to drive at night anymore because

   _____.

4. (*Our history professor is quite old.*) Our history professor is going to retire because of

   _____.

5. (*Sarah is afraid of heights.*) She will not walk across a bridge because

   _____.

6. (*Sarah is afraid of heights.*) She will not walk across a bridge because of

   _____.

7. (*There was a cancellation.*) Due to _____, you can have an

   appointment with the doctor this afternoon.

8. (*There was a cancellation today.*) Because _____, you can

   have an appointment with the doctor this afternoon.

PRACTICE 5 ▸ Cause and effect: using *therefore, consequently,* and *so*. (Chart 19-3)
Punctuate the sentences in Column B. Add capital letters if necessary.

Column A	Column B
1. adverb clause:	Because she had a headache she took some aspirin.
2. adverb clause:	She took some aspirin because she had a headache.
3. prepositional phrase:	Because of her headache she took some aspirin.
4. prepositional phrase:	She took some aspirin because of her headache.
5. transition:	She had a headache therefore she took some aspirin.
6. transition:	She had a headache she therefore took some aspirin.
7. transition:	She had a headache she took some aspirin therefore.
8. conjunction:	She had a headache so she took some aspirin.

PRACTICE 6 ▶ Cause and effect: using *therefore*, *consequently*, and *so*. (Chart 19-3)
Each sentence in *italics* is followed by sentences that refer to it. Choose the word that logically completes each sentence. Notice the punctuation and capitalization.

SENTENCE 1: *Water boils when its temperature reaches 212 degrees Fahrenheit (100 degrees Celsius).*

1. The water in the pot had reached 212 degrees Fahrenheit. _____, it started to boil.
   a. Therefore   b. So   c. Because

2. The water in the pot started to boil _____ it had reached 212 degrees Fahrenheit.
   a. so   b. because   c. therefore

3. The water in the pot had reached 212 degrees Fahrenheit, _____ it started to boil.
   a. because   b. therefore   c. so

SENTENCE 2: *The main highway is closed.*

1. The main highway is closed. _____, we are going to take another road.
   a. Therefore   b. Because   c. So

2. We are going to take another road _____ the main highway is closed.
   a. so   b. because   c. therefore

3. The main highway is closed. We are going to take another road, _____.
   a. therefore   b. Therefore   c. so

4. The main highway is closed, _____ we are going to take another road.
   a. So   b. so   c. therefore

PRACTICE 7 ▶ Cause and effect: using *therefore*, *consequently*, and *so*. (Chart 19-3)
Combine the two sentences in *italics* in four different ways. Notice the punctuation and capitalization.

1. *The store didn't have orange juice. I bought lemonade instead.*
   a. _____I bought lemonade_____ because _____the store didn't have any orange juice_____ .
   b. Because _____, _____ .
   c. _____ . Therefore, _____
      _____ .
   d. _____ , so _____ .

2. *Max has excellent grades. He will go to a top university.*
   a. _____ . Therefore, _____ .
   b. _____ . He, therefore, _____ .
   c. _____ . _____ , therefore.
   d. _____ , so _____ .

3. *There had been no rain for several months. The crops died.*
   a. Because _____ , _____ .
   b. _____ . Consequently, _____ .
   c. _____ . _____ , therefore,
      _____ .
   d. _____ , so _____ .

PRACTICE 8 ▸ Showing cause and effect. (Charts 19-2 and 19-3)

Part I. Complete the sentences with *because of*, *because*, or *therefore*. Add any necessary punctuation and capitalization.

1. _____*Because*_____ it rained we stayed home.

2. It rained. _____*Therefore,*_____ we stayed home.

3. We stayed home _____*because of*_____ the bad weather.

4. The weather was bad. _____ we stayed home.

5. The typhoon was moving directly toward a small coastal town. _____ all residents were advised to move inland until it passed.

6. The residents moved inland _____ the typhoon.

7. _____ the typhoon was moving directly toward the town all residents were advised to move inland.

8. Giraffes, which are found in the African plains, are the tallest of all animals. Although their bodies are not extremely large, they have very long necks. _____ their long necks, they are tall enough to eat the leaves from the tops of the trees.

Part II. Complete the sentence with *due to, since,* or *consequently*. Add any necessary punctuation and capitalization.

9. _____ his poor eyesight John has to sit in the front row in class.

10. _____ John has poor eyesight he has to sit in the front row.

11. John has poor eyesight _____ he has to sit in the front row.

12. Sarah is afraid of heights _____ she will not walk across a bridge.

13. Sarah will not walk across a bridge _____ her fear of heights.

14. Mark is overweight _____ his doctor has advised him to exercise regularly.

15. _____ a diamond is extremely hard it can be used to cut glass.

PRACTICE 9 ▸ Summary of patterns and punctuation. (Chart 19-4)

Punctuate the sentences properly, using periods and commas. Add capital letters if necessary.

1. Edward missed the final exam. ~~therefore~~ *Therefore,* he failed the course.

2. Edward failed the course because he missed the final exam. (*no change*)

3. Edward missed the final exam. he simply forgot to go to it.

4. Because we forgot to make a reservation we couldn't get a table at our favorite restaurant last night.

5. The server kept coming to work late or not at all therefore she was fired.

6. The server kept forgetting customers' orders so he was fired.

7. Ron is an unpleasant dinner companion because of his terrible table manners.

8. The needle has been around since prehistoric times the button was invented about 2,000 years ago the zipper wasn't invented until 1890.

9. It is possible for wildlife observers to identify individual zebras because the patterns of stripes on each zebra are unique no two zebras are alike.

10. When students in the United States are learning to type, they often practice this sentence because it contains all the letters of the English alphabet: The quick brown fox jumps over the lazy dog.

PRACTICE 10 ▶ Summary of patterns and punctuation. (Chart 19-4)
Combine the two sentences in *italics*. Use the words in parentheses in the new sentences.

SENTENCE 1: *Kim ate some bad food. She got sick.*

  a. (*because*) _____

  b. (*because of*) _____

  c. (*so*) _____

  d. (*due to*) _____

SENTENCE 2: *Adam was exhausted. He had driven for 13 hours.*

  a. (*therefore*) _____

  b. (*since*) _____

  c. (*due to the fact that*) _____

  d. (*so*) _____

PRACTICE 11 ▶ *Such ... that* and *so ... that*. (Chart 19-5)
Write **such** or **so** to complete the sentences.

  1. It was _____*such*_____ a hot day that we canceled our tennis game.

  2. The test was _____*so*_____ easy that everyone got a high score.

  3. The movie was _____ bad that we left early.

  4. It was _____ a bad movie that we left early.

  5. Professor James is _____ a demanding teacher that many students refuse to take his class.

  6. The line at the post office was _____ long that I decided to leave and go back another day.

  7. The intricate metal lacework on the Eiffel Tower in Paris was _____ complicated that the structure took more than two and a half years to complete.

  8. Charles and his brother are _____ hard-working carpenters that I'm sure they'll make a success of their new business.

  9. The kids had _____ much fun at the amusement park that they begged to go again.

  10. I feel like I have _____ little energy that I wonder if I'm getting sick.

PRACTICE 12 ▶ Using *such ... that* and *so ... that*. (Chart 19-5)
Combine the two sentences. Use **so ... that** or **such ... that**.

  1. We took a walk. It was a nice day.

    It was _____*such a nice day that we took a walk*_____.

  2. Jeff was late. He missed the meeting.

    Jeff was _____.

  3. I couldn't understand her. She talked too fast.

    She talked _____.

  4. It was an expensive car. We couldn't afford to buy it.

    It was _____.

  5. There were few people at the meeting. It was canceled.

    There were _____.

6. Ted couldn't fall asleep last night. He was worried about the exam.

Ted was _____.

7. The tornado struck with great force. It lifted cars off the ground.

The tornado _____.

8. I can't figure out what this sentence says. Joe's handwriting is illegible.

Joe's handwriting _____.

9. David has too many girlfriends. He can't remember all of their names.

David has _____.

10. Too many people came to the meeting. There were not enough seats for everyone.

There were _____.

PRACTICE 13 ▶ Expressing purpose. (Chart 19-6)

Check (✓) the sentences that express purpose.

1. _____ Ali changed jobs in order to be closer to his family.

2. _____ Ali changed jobs, so he has a lot of new information to learn.

3. _____ Ali changed jobs so he could be involved in more interesting work.

4. _____ Ali changed jobs so that he could be closer to his family.

5. _____ The highway will be closed tomorrow so that road crews can make repairs to the road.

6. _____ The highway will be closed tomorrow, so you will need to take a detour.

7. _____ The highway will be closed tomorrow so the road can be repaired.

8. _____ The highway will be closed tomorrow in order for road crews to make repairs.

9. _____ The highway will be closed tomorrow, so we can expect long delays.

10. _____ The highway will be closed tomorrow, so let's do our errands today.

PRACTICE 14 ▶ Expressing purpose: using so that. (Chart 19-6)

Complete the sentences in Column A with a clause from Column B.

Column A

1. Please open the windows so that _____.

2. Sam put on his boots so that _____.

3. I spoke softly on the phone so that _____.

4. Li bought a compact car so that _____.

5. Aiden stayed up all night so that _____.

6. You could lower the price on the house you are trying to sell so that _____.

7. The city has put up a traffic light at the busy intersection so that _____.

8. We are painting the kitchen yellow so that _____.

9. Sid wore a suit and tie for his interview so that _____.

10. Mr. Kim studies advanced Russian so that _____.

Column B

a. my roommate wouldn't wake up

b. he can be a translator

c. it will sell more quickly

d. we can have some fresh air

e. it will be safer for drivers and pedestrians

f. he would save money on gasoline

g. it will look bright and cheerful

h. he would look professional

i. he could go hiking in the mountains

j. he could finish writing his essay

PRACTICE 15 ▸ Expressing purpose: using *so that*. (Chart 19-6)
Combine the sentences by using *so* (*that*).

1. Rachel wanted to watch the news. She turned on the TV.

   Rachel turned on the TV so that she could watch the news.

2. Alex wrote down the time and date of his appointment. He didn't want to forget to go.

   _____

3. Nancy is taking extra courses every semester. She wants to graduate early.

   _____

4. Amanda didn't want to disturb her roommate. She turned down the TV.

   _____

5. Chris took some change from his pocket. He wanted to buy a snack from the vending machine.

   _____

6. I wanted to listen to the news while I was making dinner. I turned on the TV.

   _____

7. I turned off my phone. I didn't want to be interrupted while I was working.

   _____

8. It's a good idea for you to learn keyboarding skills. You'll be able to use your computer more efficiently.

   _____

9. Lynn wanted to make sure that she didn't forget to take her book back to the library. She tied a string around her finger.

   _____

10. Wastebaskets have been placed throughout the park. The department wants to make sure people don't litter.

    _____

PRACTICE 16 ▸ Showing contrast (unexpected result). (Chart 19-7)
Make logical completions by completing the sentences with *is* or *isn't*.

1. It's the middle of the summer, but the weather _____ very cold.
2. It's the middle of the summer; nevertheless, the weather _____ very cold.
3. The weather _____ warm today even though it's the middle of summer.
4. Although it's the middle of the summer, the weather _____ very cold today.
5. Even though it's the middle of summer, the weather _____ very cold today.
6. It's the middle of summer in spite of the fact that the weather _____ very warm today.
7. Despite the fact that it is the middle of summer, the weather _____ very cold today.
8. It's the middle of summer. However, the weather _____ warm today.
9. It's the middle of summer, yet the weather _____ very warm today.
10. Despite the cold weather, it _____ the middle of summer.

PRACTICE 17 ▸ *Despite, in spite of* vs. *even though, although.* (Chart 19-7)

Choose the correct completions.

1. a. Even though / Despite   her doctor has prescribed frequent exercise for her, Carol never does any exercise at all.

   b. Even though / Despite   her doctor's orders, Carol has not done any exercise at all.

   c. Even though / Despite   the orders her doctor gave her, Carol still hasn't done any exercise.

   d. Even though / Despite   the dangers of not exercising, Carol still doesn't exercise.

   e. Even though / Despite   she has been warned about the dangers of not exercising by her doctor, Carol still hasn't begun to exercise.

2. a. Although / In spite of   an approaching storm, the two climbers continued their trek up the mountain.

   b. Although / In spite of   a storm was approaching, the two climbers continued their trek.

   c. Although / In spite of   there was an approaching storm, the two climbers continued up the mountain.

   d. Although / In spite of   the storm that was approaching the mountain area, the two climbers continued their trek.

   e. Although / In spite of   the fact that a storm was approaching the mountain area, the two climbers continued their trek.

3. a. Although / Despite   his many hours of practice, George failed his driving test for the third time.

   b. Although / Despite   he had practiced for many hours, George failed his driving test for the third time.

   c. Although / Despite   practicing for many hours, George failed his driving test again.

   d. Although / Despite   his mother and father spent hours with him in the car trying to teach him how to drive, George failed his driving test repeatedly.

   e. Although / Despite   his mother and father's efforts to teach him how to drive, George failed his driving test.

4. a. Even though / In spite of   repeated crop failures due to drought, the villagers are refusing to leave their traditional homeland for resettlement in other areas.

   b. Even though / In spite of   their crops have failed repeatedly due to drought, the villagers are refusing to leave their traditional homeland for resettlement in other areas.

   c. The villagers refuse to leave   even though / in spite of   the drought.

   d. The villagers refuse to leave   even though / in spite of   the drought seriously threatens their food supply.

   e. The villagers refuse to leave   even though / in spite of   the threat to their food supply because of the continued drought.

   f. The villagers refuse to leave   even though / in spite of   the threat to their food supply is serious because of the continued drought.

   g. The villagers refuse to leave   even though / in spite of   their food supply is threatened.

   h. The villagers refuse to leave   even though / in spite of   their threatened food supply.

PRACTICE 18 ▸ Showing contrast. (Chart 19-7)
Complete each sentence with the correct phrase from the list. Write the letter.

    a. an inability to communicate well in any language besides English
    b. he had the necessary qualifications
    c. he is afraid of heights
    d. he is normally quite shy and sometimes inarticulate
    e. his fear of heights
    f. his parents were worried about his intelligence because he didn't speak until he was four years old
    g. it has been shown to be safe
    h. they have been shown to cause birth defects and sometimes death
    i. its many benefits
    j. his competence and experience

1. In spite of _____, Carl enjoyed his helicopter trip over the Grand Canyon in Arizona.

2. Although _____, Mark rode in a cable car to the top of Sugar Loaf mountain in Rio de Janeiro for the magnificent view.

3. Because of his age, John was not hired even though _____.

4. Although _____, many people avoid using a microwave oven for fear of its radiation.

5. Jack usually has little trouble making new friends in other countries despite _____.

6. In spite of _____, the use of chemotherapy to treat cancer has many severe side effects.

7. Though _____, Bob managed to give an excellent presentation at the board meeting.

8. Jerry continued to be denied a promotion despite _____.

9. Dangerous pesticides are still used in many countries even though _____.

10. Despite the fact that Einstein turned out to be a genius _____.

PRACTICE 19 ▸ Showing contrast. (Chart 19-7)
Combine the two *italicized* sentences. Add any other necessary punctuation.

1. *It was night. We could see the road very clearly.*

    a. Even though _____ .

    b. Although _____ .

    c. _____, but _____ .

2. *Helena has a fear of heights. She enjoys skydiving.*

    a. Despite the fact that _____, _____ .

    b. Despite _____, _____ .

    c. _____; nevertheless _____ .

3. *Millie has the flu. She is working at her computer.*

    a. Though _____, _____ .

    b. _____, but _____ anyway.

    c. _____, but _____ still _____
    _____ .

PRACTICE 20 ▸ Showing direct contrast. (Chart 19-8)
Connect the given ideas using the words in parentheses. Add punctuation and capital letters as necessary.

1. (*while*) red is bright and lively gray is a dull color

   _____*Red is bright and lively, while gray is a dull color.*_____ OR

   _____*While red is bright and lively, gray is a dull color.*_____

2. (*on the other hand*) Jane is insecure and unsure of herself her sister is full of self-confidence

   _____

3. (*while*) a rock is heavy a feather is light

   _____

4. (*however*) some children are unruly others are quiet and obedient

   _____

5. (*on the other hand*) language and literature classes are easy and enjoyable for Alex math and science courses are difficult for him

   _____

6. (*however*) strikes can bring improvements in wages and working conditions they can also cause loss of jobs and bankruptcy

   _____

PRACTICE 21 ▸ Expressing condition: using *otherwise*. (Chart 19-9)
Make sentences with the same meaning as the given sentence. Use ***otherwise***.

1. If I don't call my mother, she'll start worrying about me.

   _____*I should / had better / have to call my mother. Otherwise, she'll start worrying about me.*_____

2. If the bus doesn't come soon, we'll be late to work.

   _____

3. Unless you've made a reservation, you won't get seated at the restaurant.

   _____

4. If Beth doesn't stop complaining, she will lose the few friends she has.

   _____

5. You can't get on the plane unless you have a government-issued ID.

   _____

6. Louis can replace his driver's license only if he applies for it in person.

   _____

7. Only if you are a registered voter can you vote in the general election.

   _____

8. If you don't clean up the kitchen tonight, you'll have to clean it up early tomorrow.

   _____

PRACTICE 22 ▸ Expressing cause and effect. (Chart 19-9)

Complete the sentences in Column A with a phrase from Column B.

Column A

1. We see lightning first and then hear the thunder because _____ .

2. Plants need light to live. These plants didn't have light; therefore, _____ .

3. Halley's Comet appears in the sky every 76 years, so _____ .

4. Children in Scandinavia go to school in darkness in the winter since _____ .

5. Objects fall to the ground because of _____ .

6. Now that _____ , newspapers are not as necessary as they used to be.

7. People get their news faster than they used to due to _____ .

8. Because _____ , people can heat the air in a balloon and make it fly.

Column B

a. faster means of communication

b. gravity

c. hot air rises to the top

d. it will next be seen in 2061

e. light travels faster than sound

f. people can get their news instantly on the Internet

g. there is almost no daylight then

h. they died

PRACTICE 23 ▸ Expressing contrast. (Chart 19-9)

Choose the correct completions.

1. Colombia exports a lot of emeralds, while South Africa   exports / doesn't export   gold.

2. Even though Colombia exports some precious stones, it   exports / doesn't export   diamonds.

3. Although Japan   uses / doesn't use   a lot of oil, oil isn't found in Japan.

4. Despite the declining population of Japan, Tokyo's population   is / isn't   getting larger.

5. Most people believe that the pineapple is native to Hawaii, a state in the middle of the Pacific Ocean; however, pineapples   originated / didn't originate   in South America.

6. China   is / isn't   the largest producer of pineapples today. Nevertheless, Hawaii still produces a lot of pineapples.

PRACTICE 24 ▸ Expressing condition. (Chart 19-9)

Write the correct form of the verb **pass** in each sentence.

1. Keith will graduate if he ____*passes*____ all of his courses.
2. Sam won't graduate if he ____*doesn't pass*____ all of his courses.
3. Brad won't graduate unless he _____ all of his courses.
4. Joslyn will graduate only if she _____ all of her courses.
5. Jessica will graduate even if she _____ all of her courses.
6. Alex won't graduate even if he _____ all of his courses.
7. Jennifer will graduate unless she _____ all of her courses.

PRACTICE 25 ▸ Chapter review.

Complete the sentences logically using the ideas from the list. Write each verb in its correct tense. Punctuate and capitalize correctly.

a. take care of the garden (or not)
b. the flowers bloom (or not)
c. my care

1. Because I took good care of the garden, ____*the flowers bloomed*____ .
2. The flowers bloomed because ____*I took good care of the garden*____ .
3. The flowers bloomed because of ____*my care*____ .
4. The flowers didn't bloom in spite of _____ .
5. Although I took good care of the garden _____ .
6. I did not take good care of the garden therefore _____ .
7. I didn't take good care of the garden however _____ .
8. I took good care of the garden nevertheless _____ .
9. I did not take good care of the garden so _____ .
10. Even though I did not take good care of the garden _____ .
11. Since I did not take good care of the garden _____ .
12. I didn't take good care of the garden, but _____ anyway.
13. If I take good care of the garden _____ .
14. Unless I take good care of the garden _____ .
15. I must take good care of the garden otherwise _____ .
16. I did not take good care of the garden consequently _____ .
17. I did not take good care of the garden nonetheless _____ .
18. I have to take good care of the garden so that _____ .
19. Only if I take good care of the garden _____ .
20. I took good care of the garden yet _____ .
21. You'd better take good care of the garden or else _____ .
22. The flowers will probably bloom whether _____ .

CHAPTER 20

Conditional Sentences and Wishes

PRACTICE 1 ▶ Preview.
Read the passage. Underline the eight conditional clauses.

Coral Reefs

If you have ever been snorkeling or scuba diving, you may have seen a coral reef. Coral reefs look like rocks, but they are actually living creatures. Because reefs are so colorful and are home to such a large number of sea creatures, some people describe them as cities or rain forests of the ocean.

Unfortunately, coral reefs all around the world are dying. If a reef dies, so will a lot of the sea life around the reef. Coral reefs are an important part of the ocean food chain. They also provide shelter for many animals, such as fish, sponges, eels, jellyfish, sea stars, and shrimp. If there were no coral reefs, many species would simply not exist. If these creatures no longer existed, millions of people who depend on fish for their main food supply and livelihood would go hungry.

There are actions we can take to protect coral reefs. Pollution is one of the biggest problems for all sea life. If we choose to walk or bike instead of driving cars, there will be fewer pollutants. Another major problem is overfishing. If governments restrict or limit fishing around reefs, the reefs might have a chance of survival. Most importantly, we need to raise awareness. If more people were aware of the dangers of dying reefs, the reefs would probably not be in such bad condition. With greater awareness, more people will volunteer with beach and reef cleanup and be careful when swimming or diving near fragile reefs. If we follow these actions, we can keep our reefs around for future generations.

PRACTICE 2 ▶ Introduction to conditional sentences. (Chart 20-1)
Read the sentences under the given sentence. Choose *yes* if the sentence describes the situation.
Choose *no* if the sentence doesn't describe the situation.

1. If Sophie didn't have the flu, she would be at work today.

   a. Sophie has the flu.   yes no

   b. Sophie is at work today.   yes no

2. If Evan didn't take his allergy medication, he would sneeze and cough all day.

   a. Evan takes his allergy medication.   yes no

   b. Evan sneezes and coughs all day.   yes no

3. If our first flight had been on time, we would not have missed our connecting flight.

   a. The first flight was on time.   yes no

   b. We missed our connecting flight.   yes no

4. If we had a reliable car, we would drive from the East Coast to the West Coast.

    a. We have a reliable car.   yes   no

    b. We are going to drive from the East Coast to the West Coast   yes   no

    c. We would like to drive from the East Coast to the West Coast.   yes   no

5. Tim would have married Tina if she had accepted his proposal of marriage.

    a. Tina accepted Tim's marriage proposal.   yes   no

    b. Tina and Tim got married.   yes   no

    c. Tim wanted to marry Tina.   yes   no

    d. Tina wanted to marry Tim.   yes   no

PRACTICE 3 ▸ Overview of basic verb forms in conditional sentences. (Chart 20-1)
Choose the correct completions.

Group 1

   1. Present real: If it snows, __c__ .   a. I would walk to work

   2. Present unreal: If it snowed, __a__ .   b. I would have walked to work

   3. Past unreal: If it had snowed, __b__ .   c. I will walk to work

Group 2

   1. Present real: If you come early, _____ .   a. we wouldn't be late

   2. Present unreal: If you came early, _____ .   b. we wouldn't have been late

   3. Past unreal: If you had come early, _____ .   c. we won't be late

Group 3

   1. Present unreal: If Professor Smith were absent, _____ .   a. class would have been canceled.

   2. Present real: If Professor Smith is absent, _____ .   b. class will be canceled.

   3. Past unreal: If Professor Smith had been absent, _____ .   c. class would be canceled

Group 4

   1. Present real: If John finds a better job, _____ .   a. he will take it.

   2. Past unreal: If John had found a better job, _____ .   b. he would take it.

   3. Present unreal: If John found a better job, _____ .   c. he would have taken it.

PRACTICE 4 ▸ Real conditions in the present or future. (Chart 20-2)
Read the given sentence and the two sentences that follow. Complete the sentences with the verbs in the box.

be, be	forget, look	heat, boil
eat, feel	have, call	pet, purr

   1. Water boils at 100 degrees C. (212 degrees F.)

     (General truth) If you _____ water to 100 degrees C.,

     it _____ .

     (Future) If you _____ the water in that pot to 100 degrees C.,

     it _____ .

2. Sometimes I forget my own schedule.

(Habitual activity) If I _____ my schedule, I _____ at my

appointment calendar.

(Future) If I _____ my schedule tomorrow, I _____ at my

appointment calendar.

3. Sometimes the cat purrs.

(Habitual situation) If you _____ the cat gently, she _____ .

(Future) If you _____ the cat gently right now, she _____ .

4. I might have some news tomorrow.

(Future) If I _____ any news tomorrow, I _____ you.

(Habitual situation) If I _____ any news, I _____ you.

5. You eat too much junk food.

(Future) If you _____ too much junk food, you _____

energetic.

(Predictable fact) If you _____ too much junk food, you

_____ energetic.

6. It might be cloudy tonight.

(Predictable fact) If it _____ cloudy, the stars _____

visible.

(Future) If it _____ cloudy tonight, the stars _____

visible.

PRACTICE 5 ▸ Unreal (contrary to fact) in the present or future. (Chart 20-3)
Choose the sentence that describes the real situation.

1. If I had a million dollars, I would travel around the world.
   a. I have a million dollars.   b. I don't have a million dollars.

2. If I didn't have a bad cold, I'd go swimming with you.
   a. I have a bad cold.   b. I don't have a bad cold.

3. If Jenny were here, she could help us.
   a. Jenny is here.   b. Jenny isn't here.

4. If Henry weren't in charge here, nothing would ever get done.
   a. Henry is in charge here.   b. Henry isn't in charge here.

5. If I spoke Chinese, I could converse with your grandmother.
   a. I speak Chinese.   b. I don't speak Chinese.

6. If I knew the answer, I would tell you.
   a. I know the answer.   b. I don't know the answer.

PRACTICE 6 ▶ Unreal (contrary to fact) in the present or future. (Chart 20-3)
Read the given sentence(s) and the sentence that follows. Complete the second sentence with the verbs in the box.

be, be	have, go	have, travel
be, can have	have, like	like, cook

1. There aren't any trees on our street, and consequently, there is no shade.

   If there _____ trees on our street, there _____ shade.

2. We don't have enough money to travel abroad.

   If we _____ enough money, we _____ abroad.

3. The students don't have a good history teacher. They don't like history because of her.

   If the students _____ a better history teacher, they _____
   history.

4. Sam doesn't like fish, so his mother doesn't cook it for him.

   If Sam _____ fish, his mother _____ fish for him.

5. The weather is bad. We can't have our picnic at the lake today.

   If the weather _____ bad, we _____ our picnic at the lake
   today.

6. I have so much work to do. I will not go out with you tonight.

   If I _____ so much work, I _____ out with you tonight.

PRACTICE 7 ▶ Real vs. unreal in the present or future. (Charts 20-2 and 20-3)
Complete the sentences in Column A with a clause in Column B.

Column A

1. If the temperature goes below freezing, _____ .
2. If the temperature were below freezing right now, _____ .
3. If the baby is hungry, _____ .
4. If the baby were hungry, _____ .
5. If this fish were not fresh, _____ .
6. If fish is not fresh, _____ .
7. If a car runs out of gas, _____ .
8. If this car had more power, _____ .
9. If you threw a rock into the water, _____ .
10. If you throw a life ring into the water, _____ .

Column B

a. it stops
b. he cries
c. it smells bad
d. we would be very cold
e. it would go faster
f. it floats
g. it would sink
h. we will be very cold
i. it would smell bad
j. he would cry

PRACTICE 8 ▸ Unreal (contrary to fact) in the past. (Chart 20-4)
Choose the completions that describe the real situation.

1. If you had been here last night, you would have had a wonderful time. But _____.
   a. you were here   b. you weren't here

2. If I hadn't been rude, Jenna wouldn't have gotten angry. But _____.
   a. I was rude   b. I wasn't rude

3. If Anna hadn't been late, we could have seen the beginning of the movie. But _____.
   a. Anna was late   b. Anna wasn't late

4. If Rudi hadn't fallen asleep, he wouldn't have crashed into the tree. But _____.
   a. he fell asleep   b. he didn't fall asleep

5. If Alexi had studied, he might have passed the test. But _____.
   a. he studied   b. he didn't study

6. If I had known the password, I would have told you. But _____.
   a. I knew the password   b. I didn't know the password

PRACTICE 9 ▸ Unreal (contrary to fact) in the past. (Chart 20-4)
Using the information in the first sentence, complete the conditional sentences with the correct form of the verbs in parentheses.

1. Adam met his future wife, Alice, on a flight to Tokyo. (*take / meet*)

   If Adam (*not*) _____ that flight to Tokyo, he (*not*) _____

   Alice.

2. I forgot my credit card, so I couldn't pay for my groceries. (*forget / can pay*)

   If I (*not*) _____ my credit card, I _____ for my groceries.

3. I didn't know Jane was in the hospital, so I didn't visit her. (*know / visit*)

   If I _____ that Jane was in the hospital, I _____ her.

4. Alex didn't pay the electric bill. The electric company cut off his power. (*pay / cut off*)

   If Alex _____ the bill, the electric company (*not*) _____ his

   electricity.

5. The weather was bad. The outdoor concert was canceled. (*be / be*)

   If the weather _____ good, the outdoor concert

   (*not*) _____ canceled.

6. Alexander Fleming accidentally discovered the medical usefulness of a certain kind of mold.

   Scientists developed penicillin from that mold. (*discover / develop*)

   If Fleming (*not*) _____ the usefulness of that mold, scientists

   (*not*) _____ penicillin.

PRACTICE 10 ▸ Conditional sentences: present, future, or past. (Charts 20-2 → 20-4)
Complete each conversation with the correct phrase from the list. Write the letter.

a. I can join you   d. I had joined one
b. I could have joined you   e. I join one
c. I could join you   f. I joined one

1. A: Hi, Kim! Can you have lunch with us?

   B: I'm sorry, I can't. If _____, I would, but I have another appointment.

2. A: Hi, Sid! Would you like to join us for tomorrow?

   B: Maybe. I might have to work through lunch, but if _____, I will.

3. A: Hey, Mary! What happened? Why didn't you have lunch with us?

   B: Oh, if _____, I would have, but I had an emergency at my office.

4. A: Mr. Simmons, you should exercise more.

   B: I'll try, Dr. Scott. Maybe I'll join a gym. If _____, I'll get more exercise.

5. A: Ms. Mora, you need to exercise. Why don't you join a gym?

   B: Oh, Doctor, if _____, it would be a waste of money. I would never use it.

6. A: Mrs. Smith, you said you were going to join a gym, but you didn't. What happened?

   B: Right, I didn't. If _____, it would have been a waste of money. I would never have used it.

PRACTICE 11 ▶ Conditional sentences: present, future, or past. (Charts 20-2 → 20-4)
Write the correct form of the verbs in parentheses.

1. We're going to be stuck in this traffic jam for an hour. It's too bad we don't have wings. If we
   (*have*) _____ wings, we (*can, fly*) _____ over all this traffic instead
   of being stuck in it.

2. If we (*can, fly*) _____ over all this traffic, we (*get*) _____ where we
   need to be very quickly.

3. Maybe we'll get there before noon. If we (*get*) _____ there before noon, I
   (*have*) _____ a chance to talk with Olga before lunch.

4. I might have a chance to talk with Olga before we have lunch. If I (*have*) _____ a
   chance to talk with her before lunch, I (*tell*) _____ her about the job opening in
   our department.

5. I didn't have a chance to talk to John yesterday. If I (*have*) _____ a chance to talk to
   him, I (*tell*) _____ him about the job opening.

6. You didn't tell John about the job opening at the meeting yesterday. But, even if you
   (*tell*) _____ him, I'm sure that he (*be, not*) _____ interested
   at all. He wasn't looking for a new job.

PRACTICE 12 ▶ Conditional sentences. (Charts 20-2 → 20-4)
Write a conditional sentence with *if* for each given sentence.

1. I was sick yesterday, so I didn't go to class.
   If _____ *I hadn't been sick yesterday, I would have gone to class.* _____

2. Because Alan never eats breakfast, he always overeats at lunch.
   If _____

3. Kostas was late to his own wedding because his watch was slow.
   If _____

4. I don't ride the bus to work every morning because it's always so crowded.
   If _____

5. Sara didn't know that Highway 57 was closed, so she didn't take an alternative route.

   If _____

6. Camille couldn't finish unloading the truck because no one was there to help her.

   If _____

PRACTICE 13 ▶ Progressive verb forms in conditional sentences. (Chart 20-5)
Write a conditional sentence with *if* for each given sentence.

1. The wind is blowing so hard. We can't go sailing.

   _____*If the wind weren't blowing so hard, we could go sailing.*_____

2. The wind was blowing so hard. We couldn't go sailing.

   _____

3. The water is running. I can't hear you.

   _____

4. The water was running. I couldn't hear the phone.

   _____

5. The baby is hungry. That's why she's crying.

   _____

6. Jude was sleeping soundly, so he didn't hear his alarm clock.

   _____

7. I was watching an exciting mystery on TV, so I didn't answer the phone.

   _____

8. I'm trying to concentrate, so I can't talk to you now.

   _____

PRACTICE 14 ▶ Using "mixed time" in conditional sentences. (Chart 20-6)
Choose all the sentences that describe each situation.

1. If I hadn't stayed up late last night, I wouldn't be tired this morning.
   a. I went to bed late.
   b. I went to bed early.
   c. I am tired this morning.
   d. I am not tired this morning.

2. If Luke had saved some money, he could buy a house now.
   a. Luke saved some money.
   b. Luke didn't save any money.
   c. Luke can buy a house.
   d. Luke can't buy a house.

3. If I hadn't apologized to Ben, he would still be angry at me.
   a. I apologized to Ben.
   b. I didn't apologize to Ben.
   c. Ben is still angry at me.
   d. Ben is not angry at me anymore.

4. If I had taken Grandpa's advice, I wouldn't be in this mess now!
   a. I took Grandpa's advice.
   b. I didn't take Grandpa's advice.
   c. I am in a mess now.
   d. I am not in a mess now.

5. If Laura hadn't been wearing her seat belt, she would have been severely injured.
   a. Laura was wearing her seat belt.
   b. Laura wasn't wearing her seat belt.
   c. Laura was severely injured.
   d. Laura was not severely injured.

6. If new houses had not been built near the campgrounds, the area would still be wilderness.
   a. New houses have been built near the campgrounds.
   b. New houses have not been built near the campgrounds.
   c. The area is still wilderness.
   d. The area is not wilderness anymore.

PRACTICE 15 ▶ Using progressive forms and "mixed time" in conditional sentences. (Charts 20-5 and 20-6)

Write a conditional sentence with *if* for each given sentence.

1. It is raining, so we won't finish the game.

   _____*If it weren't raining, we would finish the game.*_____

2. I didn't eat lunch, and now I'm hungry.

   If _____

3. Bob left his wallet at home this morning, and now he doesn't have money for lunch.

   If _____

4. Bryce is always daydreaming, so he never gets his work done.

   If _____

5. My muscles hurt today because I played basketball for three hours last night.

   If _____

6. I couldn't hear what you said because the band was playing so loud.

   If _____

7. Because Diana asked the technician a lot of questions, she understands how to fix her computer now.

   If _____

8. Sasha and Ivan weren't paying attention, so they didn't see the exit sign on the highway.

   If _____

9. I really don't know what the test results mean because the doctor didn't explain them to me.

   If _____

10. We were sleeping last night, so we didn't feel the earthquake.

    If _____

PRACTICE 16 ▸ Omitting *if.* (Chart 20-7)

Write sentences with the same meaning by omitting *if*.

1. If I were you, I wouldn't go there.

   _____*Were I you,*_____ I wouldn't go there.

2. If you should need my help, please call.

   _____*Should you need*_____ my help, please call.

3. If I had known about her accident, I would have gone to the hospital immediately.

   _____ about her accident, I would have gone to the hospital immediately.

4. If I had been offered a job at the law office, I would have gladly accepted.

   _____ a job at the law office, I would have gladly accepted.

5. If anyone should call, would you please take a message?

   _____, would you please take a message?

6. (Directions on the pizza box) "If this pizza needs reheating, place it in a hot oven for five minutes."

   _____, place it in a hot oven for five minutes.

7. (Directions on a medicine bottle) "If you feel any dizziness, nausea, or muscle pain, discontinue taking this medicine and call your doctor immediately."

   _____ any dizziness, nausea, or muscle pain, discontinue taking this medicine and call your doctor immediately.

8. If you were really a lawyer, I would take your advice.

   _____, I would take your advice.

PRACTICE 17 ▸ Omitting *if.* (Chart 20-7)

Choose the one sentence that has the same meaning as the given sentence.

1. Had she not been texting and walking, she wouldn't have tripped and fallen down.
   a. She had to text and walk.
   b. She was texting and walking.
   c. She didn't trip.
   d. She has to text and fall down.

2. Should you have further questions, please don't hesitate to contact us again.
   a. You should ask more questions.
   b. You might have more questions.
   c. You will certainly have more questions.
   d. Don't bother calling us again.

3. Had the building been properly built, it would have withstood the hurricane.
   a. The building was properly built.
   b. The building survived the hurricane.
   c. The building wasn't properly built.
   d. The building was built after the hurricane.

4. If you were rich, you could fly across the ocean to visit your family every week.
   a. Are you rich?
   b. You are not rich.
   c. You visit your family every week.
   d. You used to be rich, but you are not anymore.

5. Had I known how much work would be involved, I never would have remodeled my kitchen.
   a. I expected it to be a lot of work.
   b. I remodeled my kitchen.
   c. I didn't remodel my kitchen.
   d. I knew how much work would be involved.

PRACTICE 18 ▸ Implied conditions. (Chart 20-8)
Rewrite the sentences with *if*-clauses.

1. Sara's dad would have picked her up, but I forgot to tell him that she needed a ride.

   Sara's dad would have picked her up if _____ *I hadn't forgotten to tell him that she needed a ride.*

2. I couldn't have finished the project without your help.

   I couldn't have finished the project if _____.

3. I opened the door slowly. Otherwise, I could have hit someone.

   If _____, I could have hit

   someone.

4. Dave would have gone on vacation with me, but he couldn't get time off from work.

   Dave would have gone with me if _____.

5. CAROL: Why didn't Oscar tell his boss about the problem?

   ALICE: He would have gotten into a lot of trouble.

   Oscar would have gotten into a lot of trouble if _____

   _____.

PRACTICE 19 ▸ Review: conditional sentences. (Charts 20-1 → 20-8)
Choose the correct completions.

1. If I spoke Spanish, I _____ abroad in Spain next year.
   a. will study   c. had studied
   b. would have studied d. would study

2. It would have been a much more serious accident _____ fast at the time.
   a. had she been driving   c. she had driven
   b. was she driving   d. if she drove

3. A: Can I borrow your car for this evening?

   B: Sure, but Nora's using it right now. If she _____ it back in time, you're welcome to borrow it.
   a. brought   c. brings
   b. would bring   d. will bring

4. I didn't get home until well after midnight last night. Otherwise, I _____ your call.
   a. returned   c. would return
   b. had returned d. would have returned

5. If energy _____ inexpensive and unlimited, many things in the world would be different.
   a. is   c. were
   b. will be   d. would be

6. We _____ the game if we'd had a few more minutes.
   a. will win   c. had won
   b. won   d. could have won

7. I _____ William with me if I had known you and he didn't get along with each other.
   a. hadn't brought   c. wouldn't have brought
   b. didn't bring   d. won't bring

8. Dr. Mason was out of town, so a guest lecturer gave the talk. It was boring and I almost fell asleep.

   If Dr. Mason _____, I would have paid attention and not fallen asleep.
   a. lectured
   b. had been lecturing
   c. was lecturing
   d. would lecture

9. If you _____ to my advice in the first place, you wouldn't be in so much trouble right now.
   a. listen
   b. had listened
   c. will listen
   d. listened

10. _____ interested in that subject, I would try to learn more about it.
    a. Were I
    b. Should I
    c. I was
    d. If I am

11. If I _____ the problems you had as a child, I might not have succeeded in life as well as you have.
    a. have
    b. would have
    c. had had
    d. should have

12. I _____ your mother to dinner if I had known she was visiting you.
    a. invite
    b. invited
    c. had invited
    d. would have invited

13. _____ more help, I can call my neighbor.
    a. Needed
    b. Should I need
    c. I have needed
    d. I should need

14. _____ then what I know today, I would have saved myself a lot of time and trouble over the years.
    a. If I know
    b. Did I know
    c. If I would know
    d. Had I known

15. Do you think there would be less conflict in the world if all people _____ the same language?
    a. speak
    b. will speak
    c. spoke
    d. had spoken

16. If you can tell me why I wasn't included, _____ this incident again.
    a. I don't mention
    b. I will never mention
    c. I never mention
    d. will I never mention

17. I didn't know you were asleep. Otherwise, I _____ so much noise when I came in.
    a. didn't make
    b. wouldn't have made
    c. won't make
    d. don't make

18. Unless you _____ all of my questions, I can't do anything to help you.
    a. answered
    b. answer
    c. would answer
    d. are answering

19. Had you told me that this was going to happen, I _____ it.
    a. never would have believed
    b. don't believe
    c. hadn't believed
    d. can't believe

20. If Jake _____ to go on the trip, would you have gone alone?
    a. doesn't agree
    b. didn't agree
    c. hadn't agreed
    d. wouldn't agree

PRACTICE 20 ▶ Wishes about the present and past. (Chart 20-9)
Choose the sentence that describes the real situation.

1. I wish that you were my true friend.
   a. You are my true friend.
   b. You are not my true friend.

2. I wish I had known the truth.
   a. I knew the truth.
   b. I didn't know the truth.

3. I wish you hadn't lied to me.
   a. You lied to me.
   b. You didn't lie to me.

4. I wish we were going on vacation.
   a. We are going on vacation.
   b. We are not going on vacation.

5. I wish I had a motorcycle.
   a. I have a motorcycle.
   b. I don't have a motorcycle.

6. I wish John could have met my father.
   a. John was able to meet my father.
   b. John was not able to meet my father.

PRACTICE 21 ▸ Wishes about the present and the past. (Chart 20-9)
Make wishes. Complete the sentences with a verb.

1. The sun isn't shining.

   I wish the sun _____*were shining*_____ right now.

2. You didn't go to the concert with us last night.

   I wish you _____ with us to the concert last night.

3. Spiro didn't drive to this party.

   I wish Spiro _____ to the party. I'd ask him for a ride home.

4. I can't swim.

   I wish I _____ so I would feel safe in a boat.

5. Our team didn't win.

   I wish our team _____ the game last night.

6. Bill didn't get the promotion.

   I wish Bill _____ the promotion. He feels bad.

7. I quit my job.

   I wish I _____ my job until I'd found another one.

8. It isn't winter.

   I wish it _____ winter so that I could go skiing.

PRACTICE 22 ▸ Verb forms following *wish*. (Chart 20-9)
Write the correct form of the verbs in parentheses.

1. Heinrich doesn't like his job as a house painter. He wishes he (*go*) _____ to art
   school when he was younger. He wishes he (*can, paint*) _____ canvasses instead
   of houses for a living.

2. I don't like living here. I wish I (*move, not*) _____ to this
   big city. I can't seem to make any friends, and everything is so crowded. I wish I
   (*take*) _____ the job I was offered before I moved here.

3. I know I shouldn't eat junk food every day, but I wish you (*stop*) _____

   nagging me about it.

4. I wish you (*invite, not*) _____ the neighbors over for dinner when you

   talked to them earlier this afternoon. I don't feel like cooking a big dinner.

5. A: Did you get your car back from the garage?

   B: Yes, and it still isn't fixed. I wish I (*pay, not*) _____ them in full when I

   picked the car up. I should have waited to make sure that everything was all right.

6. A: I wish you (*hurry*) _____! We're going to be late.

   B: I wish you (*relax*) _____. We've got plenty of time.

7. A: How do you like the new apartment manager?

   B: Not much. I wish she (*choose, not*) _____.

   A: Me too. She's not very helpful. I wish the owners (*pick*) _____

   someone else.

8. A: My thirteen-year-old daughter wishes she (*be, not*) _____ so tall and that her

   hair (*be*) _____ black and straight.

   B: Really? My daughter wishes she (*be*) _____ taller and that her hair

   (*be*) _____ blond and curly.

9. A: I can't go to the game with you this afternoon.

   B: Really? That's too bad. But I wish you (*tell*) _____ me sooner so that I

   could have invited someone else to go with me.

10. A: How long have you been sick?

    B: For over a week.

    A: I wish you (*go*) _____ to see a doctor later today. You should find out what's

    wrong with you.

    B: Maybe I'll go tomorrow.

PRACTICE 23 ▸ Wishes about the future. (Chart 20-10)
Make wishes about the future using the verbs in the box.

cook	end	get	hang up	leave	snow

1. A: So, Mom, how do you like my haircut?

   B: You got a haircut? Your hair is still long. I wish you _____ a real haircut.

2. A: Aren't you going on your annual ski trip this year?

   B: No, not unless it snows. There hasn't been any snow this year. I wish it

   _____ so we could go skiing.

3. A: Helen! How long are our guests going to stay? It's almost midnight.

   B: I don't know. I wish they _____, but Henry just keeps on talking. Everyone

   is falling asleep.

4. A: I love you, Pat, but I wish you were neater.

   B: Neater? What do you mean? I pick up everything, I clean up everything ...

   A: Well, I mean I wish you _____ your clothes instead of leaving them
      on a chair.

5. A: What's the matter? Don't you like the movie?

   B: Not at all! I wish it _____. We have to stay, though because the kids are
      enjoying it so much.

6. A: Meatballs again?

   B: Don't you like meatballs?

   A: You know I do, but sometimes I wish you _____ something else.

PRACTICE 24 ▸ Wishes about the past, present, and future. (Charts 20-9 and 20-10)
Complete the sentences with the correct form of the verbs in parentheses.

At the Pet Store

LAILA: Look at these puppies! They're so cute. I wish my apartment manager

(*allow*) _____ dogs.

REAGAN: Really? I have a dog, but I wish I (*get*) _____ a cat instead. Dogs

need a lot of attention. You have to play with them and take them for walks every day.

I go to school all day and work in the evenings, so my dog gets very lonely. I wish I

(*think*) _____ of that before. I feel guilty now.

LAILA: Don't cats need attention too?

REAGAN: Of course, but not nearly as much as dogs. Cats can take care of themselves a lot of the time.

Does your apartment manager allow cats?

LAILA: Yes, cats are allowed, but I live with my sister. She's allergic to cats. I wish she

(*have*) _____ so many allergies.

REAGAN: Yeah, that's too bad. Hey, look at all these colorful fish! They're beautiful. I wish I

(*get*) _____ a big aquarium and fill it with lots of fish, but I already have

more responsibilities than I can take care of.

LAILA: Maybe, I'll get some fish. It's not the same as a cuddly cat or dog, but it's better than nothing.

REAGAN: I really wish someone (*take*) _____ my dog for walks on the days when I'm

too busy. Would you be interested?

LAILA: I'd love to!

PRACTICE 25 ▶ Chapter review.

Complete the sentences with the correct form of the verb in parentheses.

RYAN: What's wrong, Gavin? You look awful!

GAVIN: Yeah, you (look) _____ bad too if you (have) _____ a day like
       ____1____   ____2____

   mine yesterday. My car slid into a tree because the roads were icy.

RYAN: Really? What happened?

GAVIN: Well, I guess if I (drive, not) _____ so fast,
                          _____3_____

   I (slide, not) _____ into the tree.
               ____4____

RYAN: Seriously? Speeding again, Gav? Don't you know that if a driver (step) _____
                                                                                ____5____

   on the gas on ice, the car will spin around in a circle?

GAVIN: I know that now, but I didn't know that yesterday! If I (know) _____ that
                                                                     ____6____

   yesterday, I (not, crash) _____ . And if that weren't bad enough,
                          ____7____

   I didn't have my driver's license with me, so I'll have to pay an extra fine for that when I go to

   court next month.

RYAN: You were driving without your license? Are you crazy?

GAVIN: Yeah. It fell out of my pocket.

RYAN: You sure have bad luck! If you (lose, not) _____ your wallet, you
                                                ____8____

   (have) _____ your driver's license with you when you hit a
        ____9____

   tree. If you (have) _____ your license with you, you (have to pay, not)
                     ____10____

   _____ a steep fine when you go to court next week. And of course,
   ____11____

   if you hadn't been driving too fast, you (run into, not) _____ a tree,
                                                          ____12____

   and you (be, not) _____ in this awful situation now. If I
                  ____13____

   (be) _____ you, I (take) _____ it easy and just
      ____14____   ____15____

   (stay) _____ home where you'll be no danger to yourself or to anyone else.
        ____16____

GAVIN: Yeah, thanks for the advice. Enough about me! How about you?

RYAN: Everything's going pretty well. I'm planning to take off for Florida soon. I'm sick of all this cold,

   rainy weather. I (stay) _____ here for vacation if the weather
                         ____17____

   (be, not) _____ so bad. But I need some sun!
          ____18____

GAVIN: I wish I (can, go) _____ with you. How are you planning on getting there?
                       ____19____

RYAN: If I have enough money, I (fly) _____ . Otherwise,
                                    ____20____

   I (take) _____ the bus. I wish I (can, drive) _____ my
          ____21____   ____22____

   own car there because it (be) _____ nice to have it to drive around in once I
                              ____23____

   get there, but it's such a long trip. I wish I (have) _____ someone to go with me
                                                        ____24____

   and share the driving.

GAVIN: Hey, what about me? Why don't I go with you? I can share the driving. I'm a great driver!

RYAN: Didn't you just get through telling me that you'd wrapped your car around a tree?

Appendix
Supplementary Grammar Units

PRACTICE 1 ▸ Subjects, verbs, and objects. (Chart A-1)
Underline and identify the subject (**s**), verb (**v**), and object of the verb (**o**) in each sentence.

        s   **v**   **o**
1. Airplanes have wings.
2. The teacher explained the problem.
3. Children enjoy games.
4. Jack wore a blue suit.
5. Some animals eat plants. Some animals eat other animals.
6. According to an experienced waitress, you can carry full cups of coffee without spilling them just by never looking at them.

PRACTICE 2 ▸ Transitive vs. intransitive verbs. (Chart A-1)
Underline and identify the verb in each sentence. Write **vt** if it is transitive. Write **vi** if it is intransitive.

            vi
1. Alice arrived at six o'clock.

           vt
2. We drank some tea.
3. I agree with you.
4. I waited for Sam at the airport for two hours.
5. They're staying at a resort hotel in San Antonio, Texas.
6. Mr. Chan is studying English.
7. The wind is blowing hard today.
8. I walked to the theater, but Janice rode her bicycle.
9. Crocodiles hatch from eggs.
10. Rivers flow toward the sea.

PRACTICE 3 ▸ Adjectives and adverbs. (Charts A-2 and A-3)
Underline and identify the adjectives (**adj**) and adverbs (**adv**) in these sentences.

        adj   **adv**
1. Jack opened the heavy door slowly.
2. Chinese jewelers carved beautiful ornaments from jade.
3. The old man carves wooden figures skillfully.
4. A busy executive usually has short conversations on the telephone.
5. The young woman had a very good time at the picnic yesterday.

PRACTICE 4 ▶ Adjectives and adverbs. (Charts A-2 and A-3)

Complete each sentence with the correct adjective or adverb.

1. *quick, quickly*   We ate _____quickly_____ and ran to the theater.

2. *quick, quickly*   We had a _____quick_____ dinner and ran to the theater.

3. *polite, politely*   I've always found Fred to be a _____ person.

4. *polite, politely*   He responded to my question _____ .

5. *regular, regularly*   Mr. Thomas comes to the store _____ for cheese and bread.

6. *regular, regularly*   He is a _____ customer.

7. *usual, usually*   The teacher arrived at the _____ time.

8. *usual, usually*   She _____ comes to class five minutes before it begins.

9. *good, well*   Jennifer Cooper paints _____ .

10. *good, well*   She is a _____ artist.

11. *gentle, gently*   A _____ breeze touched my face.

12. *gentle, gently*   A breeze _____ touched my face.

13. *bad, badly*   The audience booed the actors' _____ performance.

14. *bad, badly*   The audience booed and whistled because the actors performed

    _____ throughout the show.

PRACTICE 5 ▶ Midsentence adverbs. (Chart A-3)

Put the adverb in parentheses in its usual midsentence position.

1. (*always*)   Ana ^always^ takes a walk in the morning.

2. (*always*)   Tim is a hard worker.

3. (*always*)   Beth has worked hard.

4. (*always*)   Carrie works hard.

5. (*always*)   Do you work hard?

6. (*usually*)   Taxis are available at the airport.

7. (*rarely*)   Yusef takes a taxi to his office.

8. (*often*)   I have thought about quitting my job and sailing to Alaska.

9. (*probably*)   Yuko needs some help.

10. (*ever*)   Have you attended the show at the Museum of Space?

11. (*seldom*)   Brad goes out to eat at a restaurant.

12. (*hardly ever*)   The students are late.

13. (*usually*)   Do you finish your homework before dinner?

14. (*generally*)   In India, the monsoon season begins in April.

15. (*usually*)   During the monsoon season, Mr. Singh's hometown receives around 610 centimeters

    (240 inches) of rain, which is an unusually large amount.

PRACTICE 6 ▶ Identifying prepositions. (Chart A-4)

<u>Underline</u> the prepositions.

1. Jim came to class <u>without</u> his books.

2. We stayed at home during the storm.

3. Sonya walked across the bridge over the Cedar River.

4. When Alex walked through the door, his little sister ran toward him and put her arms around his neck.

5. The two of us need to talk to Tom too.

6. Animals live in all parts of the world. Animals walk or crawl on land, fly in the air, and swim in the water.

7. Scientists divide living things into two main groups: the animal kingdom and the plant kingdom.

8. Asia extends from the Pacific Ocean in the east to Africa and Europe in the west.

PRACTICE 7 ▶ Sentence elements. (Charts A-1 → A-4)

<u>Underline</u> and identify the subject (**S**), verb (**V**), object (**O**), and prepositional phrases (**PP**) in the following sentences.

       S   **V**   **O**   **PP**
1. <u>Harry</u> <u>put</u> the <u>letter</u> <u>in the mailbox</u>.

2. The kids walked to school.

3. Caroline did her homework at the library.

4. Chinese printers created the first paper money in the world.

5. Dark clouds appeared on the horizon.

6. Rhonda filled the shelves of the cabinet with boxes of old books.

PRACTICE 8 ▶ Preposition combinations. (Chart A-5)

Choose <u>all</u> the correct completions for each sentence.

1. Max is known for his (*honesty* / *fairness* / *famous*).

2. Several students were absent from (*yesterday* / *school* / *class*).

3. Has Maya recovered from (*her illness* / *her husband's death* / *the chair*)?

4. The criminal escaped from (*jail* / *the key* / *prison*).

5. Do you believe in (*ghosts* / *UFOs* / *scary*)?

6. Anthony is engaged to (*my cousin* / *a friend* / *marriage*).

7. Chris excels in (*mathematics* / *sports* / *his cousins*).

8. I'm very fond of (*you* / *exciting* / *your children*).

9. Henry doesn't approve of (*smoking* / *cigarettes* / *rain*).

10. I subscribe to (*magazines* / *a newspaper* / *websites*).

PRACTICE 9 ▶ Preposition combinations. (Chart A-5)

Choose the correct prepositions in parentheses.

1. Water consists (*of* / *with*) oxygen and hydrogen.

2. I am uncomfortable because that man is staring (*to* / *at*) me.

3. Ella hid the candy (*from* / *back*) the children.

4. I arrived (*in* / *to*) this country two weeks ago.

5. We arrived (*to* / *at*) the airport ten minutes late.

6. I am envious (*in* / *of*) people who can speak three or four languages fluently.

7. The students responded (*at* / *to*) the teacher's questions.

8. The farmers are hoping (*on* / *for*) rain.

9. I'm depending (*on* / *in*) you to finish this work for me.

10. Tim wore sunglasses to protect his eyes (*for* / *from*) the sun.

PRACTICE 10 ▸ Preposition combinations. (Chart A-5)
Complete the sentences with appropriate prepositions.

SITUATION 1: Mr. and Mrs. Jones just celebrated their 50th wedding anniversary.

1. They have been married _____*to*_____ each other for 50 years.

2. They have always been faithful _____ each other.

3. They are proud _____ their marriage.

4. They are polite _____ one another.

5. They are patient _____ each other.

6. They are devoted _____ one another.

7. They have been committed _____ their marriage.

SITUATION 2: Jacob and Emily have been together for five months. They don't have a healthy
                relationship, and it probably won't last long.

1. They are often annoyed _____ each other's behavior.

2. They argue _____ each other every day.

3. They are bored _____ their relationship.

4. They are tired _____ one another.

5. Jacob is jealous _____ Emily's friends.

6. Emily is sometimes frightened _____ Jacob's moods.

PRACTICE 11 ▸ Preposition combinations. (Chart A-5)
Complete each sentence in Column A with the correct phrase from Column B.

Column A

1. My boots are made __*c*__ .

2. We hope you succeed _____ .

3. She forgave him _____ .

4. I'm going to take care _____ .

5. The firefighters rescued many people _____ .

6. I pray _____ .

7. Trucks are prohibited _____ .

Column B

a. from the burning building

b. for telling a lie

✓ c. of leather

d. from entering the tunnel

e. in winning the scholarship

f. of the children tonight

g. for peace

PRACTICE 12 ▸ Preposition combinations. (Chart A-5)
Complete the sentences with appropriate prepositions.

1. Andrea contributed her ideas _____*to*_____ the discussion.

2. Ms. Kleeman substituted _____ our regular teacher.

3. I can't distinguish one twin _____ the other.

4. Children rely _____ their parents for food and shelter.

5. I'm worried _____ this problem.

6. I don't care _____ spaghetti. I'd rather eat something else.

7. Charles doesn't seem to care _____ his bad grades.

8. I'm afraid I don't agree _____ you.

9. We decided _____ eight o'clock as the time we should meet.

10. I am not familiar _____ that author's works.

11. Do you promise to come? I'm counting _____ you to be here.

12. The little girl is afraid _____ an imaginary bear that lives in her closet.

PRACTICE 13 ▸ Preposition combinations. (Chart A-5)
Complete the sentences with appropriate prepositions.

1. We will fight _____*for*_____ our rights.

2. Who did you vote _____ in the last election?

3. Jason was late because he wasn't aware _____ the time.

4. I am grateful _____ you _____ your assistance.

5. Elena is not content _____ the progress she is making.

6. Paul's comments were not relevant _____ the topic under discussion.

7. Have you decided _____ a date for your wedding yet?

8. Patricia applied _____ admission _____ the university.

9. Daniel dreamed _____ some of his childhood friends last night.

10. Mr. Miyagi dreams _____ owning his own business someday.

11. The accused woman was innocent _____ the crime with which she was charged.

12. Ms. Sanders is friendly _____ everyone.

13. The secretary provided me _____ a great deal of information.

14. Ivan compared the wedding customs in his country _____ those in the United States.

PRACTICE 14 ▸ Review: basic question forms. (Chart B-1)

From the underlined sentences, make questions for the given answers. Fill in the blank spaces with the appropriate words. If no word is needed, write Ø.

1. *Chris can live there.*

	Question word	Auxiliary verb	Subject	Main verb	Rest of question	→	Answer
1a.	Ø	Can	Chris	live	there ?	→	Yes.
1b.	Where	can	Chris	live	Ø ?	→	There.
1c.	Who	can	Ø	live	there ?	→	Chris.

2. *Ron is living there.*

	Question word	Auxiliary verb	Subject	Main verb	Rest of question	→	Answer
2a.	Ø				there ?	→	Yes.
2b.	Where				Ø ?	→	There.
2c.	Who				there ?	→	Ron.

3. *Kate lives there.*

	Question word	Auxiliary verb	Subject	Main verb	Rest of question	→	Answer
3a.	Ø				there ?	→	Yes.
3b.	Where				Ø ?	→	There.
3c.	Who				there ?	→	Kate.

4. *Anna will live there.*

	Question word	Auxiliary verb	Subject	Main verb	Rest of question	→	Answer
4a.	Ø				there ?	→	Yes.
4b.	Where				Ø ?	→	There.
4c.	Who				there ?	→	Anna.

5. *Jack lived there.*

	Question word	Auxiliary verb	Subject	Main verb	Rest of question	→	Answer
5a.					there ?	→	Yes.
5b.					Ø ?	→	There.
5c.					there ?	→	Jack.

6. *Mary has lived there.*

	Question word	Auxiliary verb	Subject	Main verb	Rest of question	→	Answer
6a.					?	→	Yes.
6b.					?	→	There.
6c.					?	→	Mary.

Make questions to fit the conversations. Notice in the examples that there is a short answer and then in parentheses a long answer. Your questions should produce those answers.

1. A: _____ *When are you going to the zoo?* _____

   B: Tomorrow. (*I'm going to the zoo tomorrow.*)

2. A: _____ *Are you going downtown later today?* _____

   B: Yes. (*I'm going downtown later today.*)

3. A: _____

   B: Yes. (*I live in an apartment.*)

4. A: _____

   B: In a condominium. (*Alex lives in a condominium.*)

5. A: _____

   B: Janice. (*Janice lives in that house.*)

6. A: _____

   B: Yes. (*I can speak French.*)

7. A: _____

   B: Jeff. (*Jeff can speak Arabic.*)

8. A: _____

   B: Two weeks ago. (*Ben arrived two weeks ago.*)

9. A: _____

   B: Mazzen. (*Mazzen arrived late.*)

10. A: _____

   B: The window. (*Ann is opening the window.*)

11. A: _____

   B: Opening the window. (*Ann is opening the window.*)

12. A: _____

   B: Her book. (*Mary opened her book.*)

13. A: _____

   B: Ramzy. (*Ramzy opened the door.*)

14. A: _____

   B: Yes. (*The mail has arrived.*)

15. A: _____

   B: Yes. (*I have a bicycle.*)

16. A: _____

   B: A pen. (*Zach has a pen in his hand.*)

17. A: _____

    B: Yes. (*I like ice cream.*)

18. A: _____

    B: Yes. (*I would like an ice cream cone.*)

19. A: _____

    B: A candy bar. (*Scott would like a candy bar.*)

20. A: _____

    B: Isabel. (*Isabel would like a soft drink.*)

PRACTICE 16 ▶ Information questions. (Charts B-1 and B-2)

Make questions from these sentences. The *italicized* words in parentheses should be the answers to
your questions.

1. I take my coffee (*black*). → *How do you take your coffee?*

2. I have (*an English-Spanish*) dictionary.

3. He (*runs a grocery store*) for a living.

4. Margaret was talking to (*her uncle*).

5. (*Only ten*) people showed up for the meeting.

6. (*Because of heavy fog*), none of the planes could take off.

7. She was thinking about (*her experiences as a rural doctor*).

8. I was driving (*sixty-five miles per hour*) when the police officer stopped me.

9. I like (*hot and spicy Mexican*) food best.

10. (*The*) apartment (*at the end of the hall on the second floor*) is mine.

11. Oscar is (*friendly, generous, and kindhearted*).

12. Oscar is (*tall and thin and has short black hair*).

13. (*Taylor's*) dictionary fell to the floor.

14. Abby isn't here (*because she has a doctor's appointment*).

15. All of the students in the class will be informed of their final grades (*on Friday*).

16. I feel (*awful*).

17. Of those three books, I preferred (*the one by Tolstoy*).

18. I like (*rock*) music.

19. The plane is expected to be (*an hour*) late.

20. The driver of the stalled car lit a flare (*in order to warn oncoming cars*).

21. I want (*the felt-tip*) pen, (*not the ballpoint*).

22. The weather is (*hot and humid*) in July.

23. I like my steak (*medium rare*).

24. I did (*very well*) on the test.

25. There are (*31,536,000*) seconds in a year.

PRACTICE 17 ▸ Information questions. (Charts B-1 and B-2)

Make questions from the following sentences. The words in parentheses should be the answers to your questions.

1. I need (*five dollars*). → *How much money do you need?*

2. Roberto was born (*in Panama*).

3. I go out to eat (*at least once a week*).

4. I'm waiting for (*Maria*).

5. (*My sister*) answered the phone.

6. I called (*Benjamin*).

7. (*Benjamin*) called.

8. She bought (*twelve gallons of*) gas.

9. "Deceitful" means (*"dishonest"*).

10. An abyss is (*a bottomless hole*).

11. He went (*this*) way, (*not that way*).

12. These are (*Scott's*) books and papers.

13. They have (*four*) children.

14. He has been here (*for two hours*).

15. It is (*two hundred miles*) to Madrid.

16. The doctor can see you (*at three on Friday*).

17. Her roommate is (*Jane Peters*).

18. Her roommates are (*Jane Peters and Ellen Lee*).

19. My parents have been living there (*for three years*).

20. This is (*Alice's*) book.

21. (*David and George*) are coming over for dinner.

22. Caroline's dress is (*blue*).

23. Caroline's eyes are (*brown*).

24. (*Andrew*) can't go on the picnic.

25. Andrew can't go (*because he is sick*).

26. I didn't answer the phone (*because I didn't hear it ring*).

27. I like (*classical*) music.

28. I don't understand (*the chart on page 50*).

29. Janie is (*studying*) right now.

30. You spell "sitting" (*with two "t's"—S-I-T-T-I-N-G*).

31. Xavier (*is about medium height and has red hair and freckles*).

32. Xavier is (*very serious and hard-working*).

33. Ray (*works as a civil engineer for the railroad company*).

34. Mexico is (*eight hundred miles*) from here.

35. I take my coffee (*black with sugar*).

36. Of Stockholm and Moscow, (*Stockholm*) is farther north.

37. (*Fine.*) I'm getting along (*just fine*).

PRACTICE 18 ▸ Shortened Yes/No Questions. (Chart B-3)

Make full questions from the shortened questions.

1. Find your keys? → *Did you find your keys?*

2. Want some coffee?

3. Need help?

4. Leaving already?

5. Have any questions?

6. (On an elevator) Going up?

7. Make it on time?

PRACTICE 19 ▸ Negative questions. (Chart B-4)

In these dialogues, make negative questions from the words in parentheses, and determine the expected response.

1. A: Your infected finger looks terrible. (*you, see, not*) __Haven't you seen__ a doctor yet?

   B: __No__. But I'm going to. I don't want the infection to get any worse.

2. A: You look pale. What's the matter? (*you, feel*) _____ well?

   B: _____. I think I might be coming down with something.

3. A: Did you see Mark at the meeting?

   B: No, I didn't.

   A: Really? (*he, be, not*) _____ there?

   B: _____.

   A: That's funny. I've never known him to miss a meeting before.

4. A: Why didn't you come to the meeting yesterday afternoon?

   B: What meeting? I didn't know there was a meeting.

   A: (*Dana, tell, not*) _____ you about it?

   B: _____. No one said a word to me about it.

5. A: I have a package for Jill. (*Jill and you, work, not*) _____
   _____ in the same building?

   B: _____. I'd be happy to take the package to her tomorrow when I go to work.

6. A: Kevin didn't report all of his income on his tax forms.

   B: (*that, be, not*) _____ against the law?

   A: _____. And that's why he's in a lot of legal trouble. He might even go to jail.

7. A: Did you give Miranda my message when you went to class this morning?

   B: No. I didn't see her.

   A: Oh? (*she, be*) _____ in class?

   B: _____. She didn't come today.

8. A: Do you see that woman over there, the one in the blue dress? (*she, be*) _____
   Mrs. Robbins?

   B: _____.

   A: I thought so. I wonder what she is doing here.

PRACTICE 20 ▶ Tag questions. (Chart B-5)

Add tag questions to the following.

1. You live in an apartment, ___*don't you*___?

2. You've never been in Italy, ___*have you*___?

3. Sara turned in her report, _____?

4. There are more countries north of the equator than south of it, _____?

5. You've never met Jack Freeman, _____?

6. You have a ticket to the game, _____?

7. You'll be there, _____?

8. John knows Claire Reed, _____?

9. We should call Rhonda, _____?

10. Ostriches can't swim, _____?

11. These books aren't yours, _____?

12. That's Charlie's, _____?

13. Your neighbors died in the accident, _____?

14. I'm right, _____?

15. This grammar is easy, _____?

PRACTICE 21 ▶ Contractions. (Chart C)

Write the contraction of the pronoun and verb if appropriate. Write Ø if the pronoun and verb cannot be contracted.

1. He is (__*He's*__) in my class.

2. He was (__Ø__) in my class.

3. He has (__*He's*__) been here since July.

4. He has (__Ø__) a Volvo.★

5. She had (_____) been there for a long time before we arrived.

6. She had (_____) a bad cold.

7. She would (_____) like to go to the zoo.

8. I did (_____) well on the test.

9. We will (_____) be there early.

10. They are (_____) in their seats over there.

11. It is (_____) going to be hot tomorrow.

12. It has (_____) been a long time since I've seen him.

13. A bear is a large animal. It has (_____) four legs and brown hair.★

14. We were (_____) on time.

15. We are (_____) always on time.

16. She has (_____) a good job.★

17. She has (_____) been working there for a long time.

★NOTE: **has, have,** and **had** are NOT contracted when they are used as main verbs. They are contracted only when they are used as helping verbs.

18. She had (_____) opened the window before class began.

19. She would (_____) have helped us if we had (_____) asked her.

20. He could have helped us if he had (_____) been there.

PRACTICE 22 ▸ Using *not* and *no*. (Chart D-1)
Change each sentence into the negative in two ways: use *not . . . any* in one sentence and *no* in the other.

1. I have some problems. → *I don't have any problems. I have no problems.*

2. There was some food on the shelf.

3. I received some letters from home.

4. I need some help.

5. We have some time to waste.

6. You should have given the beggar some money.

7. I trust someone. → *I don't trust anyone. I trust no one.***

8. I saw someone.

9. There was someone in his room.

10. She can find somebody who knows about it.

PRACTICE 23 ▸ Avoiding double negatives. (Chart D-2)
Correct the errors in these sentences, all of which contain double negatives.

1. We don't have no time to waste.

   → *We have no time to waste.* OR *We don't have any time to waste.*

2. I didn't have no problems.

3. I can't do nothing about it.

4. You can't hardly ever understand her when she speaks.

5. I don't know neither Joy nor her husband.

6. Don't never drink water from that river without boiling it first.

7. Because I had to sit in the back row of the auditorium, I couldn't barely hear the speaker.

PRACTICE 24 ▸ Beginning a sentence with a negative word. (Chart D-3)
Change each sentence so that it begins with a negative word.

1. I had hardly stepped out of bed when the phone rang.

   → *Hardly had I stepped out of bed when the phone rang.*

2. I will never say that again.

3. I have scarcely ever enjoyed myself more than I did yesterday.

4. She rarely makes a mistake.

5. I will never trust him again because he lied to me.

6. It is hardly ever possible to get an appointment to see him.

7. I seldom skip breakfast.

8. I have never known a more generous person than Samantha.

They're, their, and *there* all have the same pronunciation.

**Also spelled with a hyphen in British English: *no-one*

PRACTICE 25 ▸ Spelling of -ing forms. (Chart E-2)

Write the -ing form of each verb in the correct column.

	Just add -ing to the simple form.	**Drop the final -e and add -ing.**	**Double the final letter and add -ing.**
1. arrive		*arriving*	
2. copy	*copying*		
3. cut			*cutting*
4. enjoy			
5. fill			
6. happen			
7. hope			
8. leave			
9. make			
10. rub			
11. stay			
12. stop			
13. take			
14. win			
15. work			

PRACTICE 26 ▸ Spelling of -ed forms. (Chart E-2)

Write the -ed form for each verb in the correct column.

	Just add -ed to the simple form.	**Add -d only.**	**Double the final letter and add -ed.**	**Change the -y to -i and add -ed.**
1. bother	*bothered*			
2. copy				*copied*
3. enjoy				
4. snore				
5. fear				
6. occur				
7. pat				
8. play				
9. rain				
10. refer				
11. reply				
12. return				
13. scare				
14. try				
15. walk				

PRACTICE 27 ▶ The simple tenses and the progressive tenses. (Chart E-3)
Circle the correct verb to complete each sentence.

1. It (*is raining* / *rains*) every day in August.

2. Uncle Joe (*visited* / *visits*) us last month.

3. Our team (*will win* / *wins*) the soccer game tomorrow.

4. Nick (*watches* / *is watching*) an action movie on TV now.

5. Tomorrow at this time we (*will be flying* / *are flying*) over the Atlantic Ocean.

6. Tina! I (*was thinking* / *am thinking*) of you just a minute ago when the phone rang!

7. I know you, Aunt Martha. You're never going to retire. You (*are working* / *will be working*) at your computer even when you are 90 years old.

8. At 9:00 P.M. last night, all the children (*go* / *went*) to bed. At 10:00 P.M. they (*slept* / *were sleeping*).

9. Uh-oh. Look! Mr. Anton (*fell* / *was falling*) down on the ice. Mr. Anton! Don't move! We (*help* / *will help*) you!

10. A: Why is the beach closed today?

    B: There are sharks in the water! They (*swim* / *are swimming*) near the shore!

PRACTICE 28 ▶ The perfect tenses. (Chart E-3)
Circle the correct verb to complete each sentence.

1. I (*have* / *had*) already seen the movie twice.

2. I (*have* / *had*) already seen the movie, so I didn't want to see it again.

3. Matthew (*has been* / *was*) a professor at this university since 2001. He's going to be chairman of the English department next year.

4. Fred (*has been* / *was*) a judge in the Supreme Court of this state for 21 years until he retired last year.

5. On the 14th of next month, my grandparents are going to celebrate their 50th wedding anniversary. They (*will have been* / *had been*) married for 50 years.

6. Rafael and Julie live in Springfield. They (*lived* / *have lived*) there all their lives.

7. Susanna and Jeff moved to Chicago. Before that, they (*have* / *had*) lived in this town all their lives.

8. Sorry, Mr. Wu. You (*have* / *will have*) missed your flight! The plane left just two minutes ago.

9. Javier speaks excellent English. He (*had* / *has*) studied English in school for twelve years before he came here.

10. We were too late to have dinner at the restaurant. When we got there, it (*has* / *had*) already closed for the night.

PRACTICE 29 ▶ The perfect progressive tenses. (Chart E-3)
Circle the correct verb to complete each sentence.

1. I'm thirsty, aren't you? We (*have* / *had*) been driving for four hours. Let's stop for a cold drink soon.

2. When is the rain going to stop? It (*has been* / *was*) raining for two days.

3. When Greta graduates from medical school next year, she (*will be / will have been*) studying for twenty years!

4. After Jim and Kim (*have / had*) been going out together for seven years, they finally got married last month.

5. You (*has / have*) been working in this office for only two months, and you've already gotten a raise? That's great!

6. Stan finally quit playing professional tennis after he broke his ankle two months ago. He (*has / had*) been playing for twenty years.

7. Well, it's good to be on this plane. Finally! We (*have been waiting / will have been waiting*) almost two hours!

8. Wake Maria up now. She (*had / has*) been sleeping for three hours. That's a very long nap.

9. The police officer gave Pedro a ticket because he (*has / had*) been speeding.

PRACTICE 30 ▶ Summary of verb tenses. (Charts E-4)
Write the correct form of the verbs in parentheses to complete the sentences.

	SIMPLE	**PROGRESSIVE**
PRESENT	1. Tom has regular habits. He (*eat*) _____ dinner every day. He has eaten dinner every day since he was a child. He ate dinner every day last month. He ate dinner yesterday. He will eat dinner tomorrow. He will probably eat dinner almost every day until the end of his life.	4. At 7:00 this evening, Tom started to eat dinner. It is now 7:15. Tom is on the phone because Mary called him. He says, "Can I call you back? I (*eat*) _____ dinner right now. I'll finish soon and will call you back. I don't want my dinner to get cold." Tom's dinner is in progress when Mary calls.
PAST	2. Tom eats dinner every day. Usually he eats at home, but yesterday, he (*eat*) _____ dinner at a restaurant.	5. Last week Tom went to a restaurant. He began to eat at 7:00. At 7:15 Mary came into the restaurant, saw Tom, and walked over to say hello. Tom's dinner was still in front of him. He hadn't finished it yet. In other words, when Mary walked into the restaurant, Tom (*eat*) _____ dinner. Tom's dinner was in progress when Mary arrived.
FUTURE	3. Tom ate dinner yesterday. He eats dinner every day. In all probability, he (*eat*) _____ dinner tomorrow.	6. Tom will begin his dinner at 7:00 tonight. Mary will arrive at 7:15. It takes Tom 30 minutes to eat his dinner. In other words, when Mary arrives tonight, Tom (*eat*) _____ his dinner. Tom's dinner will be in progress when Mary arrives.

	PERFECT	PERFECT PROGRESSIVE
PRESENT	7. Tom finished eating dinner at 7:30 tonight. It is now 8:00, and his mother has just come into the kitchen. She says, "What would you like for dinner? Can I cook something for you?" Tom says, "Thanks Mom, but I (*eat, already*) _____ dinner."	10. Tom began to eat dinner at 7:00 tonight. It is now, at this moment, 7:15. Tom (*eat*) _____ _____ his dinner for 15 minutes, but he hasn't finished yet. In other words, his dinner has been in progress for 15 minutes.
PAST	8. Yesterday Tom cooked his own dinner. He began at 7:00 and finished at 7:30. At 8:00 his mother came into the kitchen. She offered to cook some food for Tom, but he (*eat, already*) _____. In other words, Tom had finished his dinner before he talked to his mother.	11. Last week Tom went to a restaurant. He began to eat at 7:00. At 7:15 Mary came into the restaurant, saw Tom, and walked over to say hello. Tom's dinner was still in front of him. He hadn't finished it yet. In other words, when Mary walked into the restaurant, Tom (*eat*) _____ dinner. Tom's dinner was in progress when Mary arrived.
FUTURE	9. Tomorrow Tom will begin dinner at 7:00 and finish at 7:30. His mother will come into the kitchen at 8:00. In other words, Tom (*eat, already*) _____ dinner by the time his mother walks into the kitchen.	12. Tonight Tom will go to a restaurant. He will begin to eat at 7:00. At 7:15 Mary will come into the restaurant, see Tom, and walk over to say hello. Tom's dinner will still be in front of him. He won't have finished it yet. In other words, when Mary walks into the restaurant, Tom (*eat*) _____ _____ dinner for 15 minutes. Tom's dinner will have been in progress for 15 minutes by the time Mary arrives.

PRACTICE 31 ▶ Linking verbs. (Chart E-7)
Some of the *italicized* words in the following are used as linking verbs. Identify which ones are linking verbs by underlining them. Also underline the adjective that follows the linking verb.

1. Olivia *looked* at the fruit. (*no underline*)

2. It *looked* fresh.

3. Dan *noticed* a scratch on the door of his car.

4. Morris *tasted* the candy.

5. It *tasted* good.

6. The crowd *grew* quiet as the official began her speech.

7. Felix *grows* tomatoes in his garden.

8. Bella *grew* up in Florida.

9. I can *smell* the chicken in the oven.

10. It *smells* delicious.

11. Dahlia *got* a package in the mail.

12. Allie *got* sleepy after dinner.

13. During the storm, the sea *became* rough.

14. Vanessa *became* a doctor after many years of study.

15. Diana *sounded* her horn to warn the driver of the other car.

16. Helen *sounded* happy when I talked to her.

17. The weather *turns* hot in July.

18. When Aiden entered the room, I *turned* around to look at him.

19. I *turned* a page in the book.

20. It *appears* certain that Mary Hanson will win the election.

21. Cameron's story *seems* strange. Do you believe it?

PRACTICE 32 ▸ Linking verbs; adjectives and adverbs. (Chart E-7)
Complete each sentence with the correct adjective or adverb.

1. *clean, cleanly*   The floor looks _____clean_____.

2. *slow, slowly*   The bear climbed _____slowly_____ up the tree.

3. *safe, safely*   The plane landed _____ on the runway.

4. *anxious, anxiously*   When the wind started to blow, I grew _____.

5. *complete, completely*   This list of names appears _____. No more names need to be added.

6. *wild, wildly*   The crowd yelled _____ when we scored a goal.

7. *honest, honestly*   The clerk looked _____, but she wasn't. I discovered when I got home that she had cheated me.

8. *thoughtful, thoughtfully*   Jane looked at her book _____ before she answered the teacher's question.

9. *good, well*   Most of the students did _____ on their tests.

10. *fair, fairly*   The contract offer sounded _____ to me, so I accepted the job.

11. *terrible, terribly*   Jim felt _____ about forgetting his son's birthday.

12. *good, well*   A rose smells _____.

13. *light, lightly*   As dawn approached, the sky became _____.

14. *confident, confidently*   Kennedy spoke _____ when she delivered her speech.

15. *famous, famously*   The actor became _____ throughout much of the world.

16. *fine, finely*   I don't think this milk is spoiled. It tastes _____ to me.

PRACTICE 33 ▸ Troublesome verbs. (Chart E-8)
Choose the correct verb in parentheses.

1. The student (*raised*/ *rose*) his hand in class.

2. Hot air (*raises / rises*).

3. Natasha (*set / sat*) in a chair because she was tired.

4. I (*set / sat*) your dictionary on the table a few minutes ago.

5. Hens (*lay / lie*) eggs.

6. Sara is (*laying / lying*) on the grass in the park right now.

7. Jan (*laid / lay*) the comb on top of the dresser a few minutes ago.

8. If you are tired, you should (*lay / lie*) down and take a nap.

9. San Francisco (*lays / lies*) to the north of Los Angeles.

10. Mr. Faust (*raises / rises*) many different kinds of flowers in his garden.

11. The student (*raised / rose*) from her seat and walked to the front of the auditorium to receive her diploma.

12. Hiroki is a very methodical person. Every night before going to bed, he (*lays / lies*) his clothes for the next day on his chair.

13. Where are my keys? I (*lay / laid*) them here on the desk five minutes ago.

14. Fahad (*set / sat*) the table for dinner.

15. Fahad (*set / sat*) at the table for dinner.

16. The fulfillment of all your dreams (*lies / lays*) within you — if you just believe in yourself.

Special Workbook Section

Phrasal Verbs

PHRASAL VERBS (TWO-WORD AND THREE-WORD VERBS)

The term *phrasal verb* refers to a verb and particle which together have a special meaning. For example, ***put + off*** means "postpone." Sometimes a phrasal verb consists of three parts. For example, ***put + up + with*** means "tolerate." Phrasal verbs are also called *two-word verbs* or *three-word verbs*.

SEPARABLE PHRASAL VERBS (a) *I handed* my paper *in* yesterday. (b) *I handed in* my paper yesterday. (c) *I handed it in* yesterday. (INCORRECT: I *handed in it* yesterday.)	A phrasal verb may be either *separable* or *nonseparable*. With a separable phrasal verb, a noun may come either between the verb and the preposition or after the preposition, as in (a) and (b). A pronoun comes between the verb and the preposition if the phrasal verb is separable, as in (c).

NONSEPARABLE PHRASAL VERBS
(d) *I ran into* an old friend yesterday.
(e) *I ran into* her yesterday.
   (INCORRECT: I *ran* an old friend *into*.)
   (INCORRECT: I *ran* her *into* yesterday.)
	With a nonseparable phrasal verb, a noun or pronoun must follow the preposition, as in (d) and (e).

Phrasal verbs are especially common in informal English. Following is a list of common phrasal verbs and their usual meanings. This list contains only those phrasal verbs used in the exercises in the text. The phrasal verbs marked with an asterisk (*) are nonseparable.

A   ask out . . . . *ask someone to go on a date*

B   bring about, bring on . . . . *cause*
        bring up . . . . *(1) rear children; (2) mention or introduce a topic*

C   call back. . . . . *return a telephone call*
        call in . . . . *ask to come to an official place for a specific purpose*
        call off . . . . *cancel*
        *call on . . . . *ask to speak in class*
        call up . . . . *call on the telephone*
        *catch up (with). . . . . *reach the same position or level*
        *check in, check into . . . . *register at a hotel*
        check into. . . . . *investigate*
        check out . . . . *(1) borrow a book from the library; (2) investigate*
        check out (of). . . . . *leave a hotel*
        cheer up . . . . *make (someone) feel happier*
        clean up . . . . *make clean and orderly*
        *come across . . . . *meet / find by chance*
        cross out. . . . . *draw a line through*
        cut out . . . . *stop an annoying activity*

D   do over. . . . . *do again*
        *drop by, drop in (on) . . . . *visit informally*
        drop off . . . . *leave something / someone at a place*
        *drop out (of) . . . . *stop going to school, to a class, to a club, etc.*

F   figure out . . . . *find the answer by reasoning*
       fill out . . . . *write the answers to a questionnaire or complete an official form*
       find out . . . . *discover information*

G   *get along (with) . . . . *have a good relationship with*
       get back (from) . . . . *(1) return from a place; (2) receive again*
       *get in, get into . . . . *(1) enter a car; (2) arrive*
       *get off . . . . *leave an airplane, a bus, a train, a subway, a bicycle*
       *get on . . . . *enter an airplane, a bus, a train, a subway, a bicycle*
       *get out of . . . . *(1) leave a car; (2) avoid work or an unpleasant activity*
       get over . . . . *recover from an illness*
       get through (with) . . . . *finish*
       *get up (from) . . . . *arise from a bed, a chair*
       give back . . . . *return an item to someone*
       give up . . . . *stop trying, quit*
       *go over . . . . *review or check carefully*
       *grow up . . . . *become an adult*

H   hand in . . . . *submit an assignment*
       hang up . . . . *(1) conclude a telephone conversation; (2) put clothes on a hanger or a hook*
       have on . . . . *wear*

K   keep out (of) . . . . *not enter*
       *keep up (with) . . . . *stay at the same position or level*
       kick out (of) . . . . *force (someone) to leave*

L   *look after . . . . *take care of*
       *look into . . . . *investigate*
       *look out (for) . . . . *be careful*
       look over . . . . *review or check carefully*
       look up . . . . *look for information in a reference book, on the internet, etc.*

M   make up . . . . *(1) invent; (2) do past-due work*

N   name after, name for . . . . *give a baby the name of someone else*

P   *pass away, pass on . . . . *die*
       pass out . . . . *distribute*
       *pass out . . . . *lose consciousness*
       pick out . . . . *select*
       pick up . . . . *(1) go to get someone (e.g., in a car); (2) take in one's hand*
       point out . . . . *call attention to*
       put away . . . . *remove to a proper place*
       put back . . . . *return to the original place*
       put off . . . . *postpone*
       put on . . . . *put clothes on one's body*
       put out . . . . *extinguish a cigarette, cigar, fire*
       *put up with . . . . *tolerate*

R   *run into, *run across . . . . *meet by chance*
       *run out (of) . . . . *finish a supply of something*

S   *show up . . . . *appear, come*
       shut off . . . . *stop a machine, light, faucet*

T *take after . . . . *resemble*
take off. . . . . *(1) remove clothing; (2) leave on a trip*
take out . . . . *(1) take someone on a date; (2) remove*
take over. . . . . *take control*
take up . . . . *begin a new activity or topic*
tear down . . . . *demolish; reduce to nothing*
tear up . . . . *tear into many little pieces*
think over . . . . *consider carefully*
throw away, throw out. . . . . *discard, get rid of*
throw up. . . . . *vomit; regurgitate food*
try on . . . . *put on clothing to see if it fits*
turn down . . . . *decrease volume or intensity*
turn in . . . . *(1) submit an assignment; (2) go to bed*
turn off. . . . . *stop a machine, light, faucet*
turn on. . . . . *start a machine, light, faucet*
turn out . . . . *extinguish a light*
turn up. . . . . *increase volume or intensity*

PRACTICE 1 ▶ Phrasal verbs.

Complete each sentence with the appropriate preposition(s). The meaning of the phrasal verb is in parentheses.

1. Lara looked . . .

   a. ___*after*___ her father when he was sick. (*took care of*)

   b. _____ her children's homework. (*reviewed*)

   c. _____ some information on the Internet. (*looked for information*)

   d. _____ an unusual situation at work. (*investigated*)

2. The tourists checked . . .

   a. _____ travel DVDs from the library before their trip. (*borrowed*)

   b. _____ their hotel. (*registered at*)

   c. _____ a famous archeological site. (*investigated*)

   d. _____ _____ their hotel rooms. (*left*)

3. Mrs. Jenkins got . . .

   a. _____ a serious illness. (*recovered from*)

   b. _____ _____ her planning for her daughter's wedding. (*finished*)

   c. _____ _____ doing an unimportant project at work. (*avoided*)

   d. _____ _____ her summer vacation early. (*returned*)

   e. _____ the subway at an unfamiliar stop. (*left*)

4. The school principal called . . .

   a. _____ the school assembly. (*canceled*)

   b. _____ some parents. (*telephoned*)

   c. _____ a few students to answer questions while visiting a class. (*asked them to speak*)

   d. _____ a teacher who was sick. (*returned a phone call*)

   e. _____ a student for discipline. (*asked the student to come to his/her office*)

PRACTICE 2 ▸ Phrasal verbs.

Complete each sentence with the correct form of a phrasal verb from the list. One phrasal verb is used twice.

get along with	pass out (2)	put up with	take after	turn in
pass away	pick out	show up	think over	

1. The flight attendants gave one snack to passengers during the flight. They _passed_ _out_ small bags of peanuts.

2. You choose the vegetables for dinner. _____ _____ whatever you like.

3. You look like your mother, but your brother _____ _____ your father.

4. I have three good job offers to consider. I need some time to _____ them _____.

5. Nathan tolerates his roommate's messy habits. I wonder how he _____ _____ _____ them.

6. Mary's elderly mother died last week. She _____ _____ after a long illness.

7. Julianna was two hours late for the dinner party. When she finally appeared, her friends told her it was rude to _____ _____ so late.

8. The Smiths are a friendly couple and people really like them. They seem to _____ _____ _____ everyone.

9. Good night. It's bedtime. I'm going to _____ _____ now.

10. Hannah got hit in the head with a golf ball, but fortunately didn't lose consciousness. The ball was traveling so fast that it was a miracle she didn't _____ _____ .

PRACTICE 3 ▸ Phrasal verbs.

Choose the correct completions. More than one completion may be correct.

1. When do we turn in   our assignment?   the dinner?   yesterday?
2. Mario made up   a lie.   a story.   a flower.
3. The government took over   the city.   the banks.   the trees.
4. Please put out   your cigarette.   the lights.   the fire.
5. What brought about   the war?   the package?   the crisis?
6. Did you figure out   working?   the problem?   the puzzle?
7. How do I turn on   the lights?   the music?   the printer?
8. Hugo asked out   his classmate.   a question.   a girl.
9. Jill is going to give up   a present.   chocolate.   smoking.
10. At the airport, I came across   a friend.   a classmate.   to fly.
11. Tina dropped out of   high school.   the ball.   college.

PRACTICE 4 ▶ Phrasal verbs.

Complete each sentence with an appropriate preposition from the list to form a two-word verb. Some prepositions may be used more than once.

| back | into | off | on | out | up |

1. A: Guess who I ran ___into___ today as I was walking across campus. Ann Keefe!

   B: You're kidding!

2. A: There will be a test on Chapters 8 and 9 next Friday.

   B: Oh, no! Couldn't you put it _____ until Monday?

3. A: You'd better put _____ your coat before you leave. It's chilly out.

   B: What's the temperature?

4. A: I smell something burning in the kitchen. Can I call you _____ in a minute?

   B: Sure. I hope your dinner hasn't burned.

   A: So do I! Bye.

5. A: I think that if I learn enough vocabulary I won't have any trouble using English.

   B: That's not necessarily so. I'd like to point _____ that language consists of much more than just vocabulary.

6. A: Your children certainly love the outdoors.

   B: Yes, they do. We brought them _____ to appreciate nature.

7. A: What forms do I have to fill out to change my tourist visa to a student visa?

   B: I don't know, but I'll look _____ it first thing tomorrow and try to find _____. I'll let you know.

8. A: How long were you in the hospital?

   B: About a week. But I've missed almost two weeks of classes.

   A: It's going to be hard for you to make _____ all the work you've missed, isn't it?

   B: Very.

9. A: Could you pick _____ a newspaper on your way home from work tonight? There's a story I want to read.

   B: Sure.

10. A: I like your new shoes.

    B: Thanks. I had to try _____ almost a dozen pairs before I decided to get these.

PRACTICE 5 ▶ Phrasal verbs.

Complete each sentence with an appropriate preposition from the list to form a two-word verb. Some prepositions may be used more than once.

| about | away | in | of | off | on | out | up |

1. A: I'm trying to find yesterday's newspaper. Have you seen it?
   B: I'm afraid I threw it ___*away / out*___. I thought you had finished reading it.

2. A: Where did you grow _____?
   B: In Seattle, Washington.

3. A: Don't forget to turn the lights _____ before you go to bed.
   B: I won't.

4. A: I have a car, so I can drive us to the festival.
   B: Good.
   A: What time should I pick you _____?
   B: Any time after five would be fine.

5. A: We couldn't see the show at the outdoor theater last night.
   B: Why not?
   A: It was called _____ on account of rain.

6. A: Thomas looks sad.
   B: I think he misses his girlfriend. Let's try to cheer him _____.

7. A: What brought _____ your decision to quit your present job?
   B: I was offered a better job.

8. A: Why did you come back early from your trip?
   B: Unfortunately, I ran _____ _____ money.

9. A: Thanks for the ride. I appreciate it.
   B: Where should I drop you _____?

10. A: What time does your plane take _____?
    B: 10:40.
    A: How long does the flight take?
    B: I think we get _____ around 12:30.

PRACTICE 6 ▶ Phrasal verbs.

Complete the sentences with appropriate prepositions to form two-word or three-word verbs.

1. A: Look ___*out*___! A car is coming!

2. A: May I borrow your dictionary?
   B: Sure. But please be sure to put it _____ on the shelf when you're finished.

3. A: I'm going to be in your neighborhood tomorrow.
   B: Oh? If you have time, why don't you drop _____ to see us?

4. A: How does this tape recorder work?

   B: Push this button to turn it _____ and push that button to shut it _____.

5. A: Did you hear what started the forest fire?

   B: Yes. Some campers built a fire, but when they left their campsite, they didn't _____ it _____ completely.

6. A: I need to talk to Karen.

   B: Why don't you call her _____? She's probably at home now.

7. A: Uh-oh. I made a mistake on the check I just wrote.

   B: Don't try to correct the mistake. Just tear _____ the check and throw it _____.

8. A: Are you here to apply for a job?

   B: Yes.

   A: Here is an application form. Fill it _____ and then give it _____ to me when you are finished.

9. A: Look. There's Mike.

   B: Where?

   A: At the other end of the block, walking toward the administration building. If we run, we can catch _____ with him.

10. A: Is your roommate here?

    B: Yes. She decided to come to the party after all. Have you ever met her?

    A: No, but I'd like to.

    B: She's the one standing over there by the far window. She has a blue dress _____. Come on. I'll introduce you.

PRACTICE 7 ▸ Phrasal verbs.
Complete each sentence with an appropriate preposition.

1. A: What time did you get _____*up*_____ this morning?

   B: I slept late. I didn't drag myself out of bed until after nine.

2. A: How did you do on your composition?

   B: Not well. It had a lot of spelling mistakes, so I have to do it _____.

3. A: What's the baby's name?

   B: Helen. She was named _____ her paternal grandmother.

4. A: I need to get more exercise.

   B: Why don't you take _____ tennis?

5. A: You can't go in there.

   B: Why not?

   A: Look at that sign. It says, "Keep _____. No trespassing."

6. A: The radio is too loud. Would you mind if I turned it _____ a little?

   B: No.

7. A: I can't hear the radio. Could you turn it _____ a little?

   B: Sure.

8. A: What are you doing Saturday night, Bob?

   B: I'm taking Virginia _____ for dinner and a show.

9. A: Don't you think it's hot in here?

   B: Not especially. If you're hot, why don't you take your sweater _____?

10. A: How do you spell *occasionally*?

    B: I'm not sure. You'd better look it _____ in your dictionary.

11. A: I'm tired. I wish I could get _____ of going to the meeting tonight.

    B: Why do you have to go?

PRACTICE 8 ▶ Phrasal verbs.

Complete each sentence with an appropriate preposition.

1. A: I need my dictionary, but I lent it to José.

   B: Why don't you get it ____*back*____ from him?

2. A: Cindy is only three. She likes to play with the older kids, but when they're running and playing, she can't keep _____ with them.

   B: She doesn't seem to mind, does she?

3. A: I made a mistake in my composition. What should I do?

   B: Since it's an in-class composition, just cross it _____.

4. A: What happened when the pilot of the plane passed out during the flight?

   B: The co-pilot took _____.

5. I took a plane from Atlanta to Miami. I got _____ the plane in Atlanta. I got _____ the plane in Miami.

6. It was a snowy winter day, but I still had to drive to work. First I got _____ the car to start the engine. Then I got _____ of the car to scrape the snow and ice from the windows.

7. Last year I took a train trip. I got _____ the train in Chicago. I got _____ the train in Des Moines.

8. Jessica takes the bus to work. She gets _____ the bus at Lindbergh Boulevard and gets _____ the bus about two blocks from her office on Tower Street.

9. A: Do you like living in the dorm?

 B: It's OK. I've learned to put _____ _____ all the noise.

10. A: What brought _____ your decision to quit your job?

 B: I couldn't get _____ _____ my boss.

11. A: Did you go _____ your paper carefully before you handed it _____ ?

 B: Yes. I looked it _____ carefully.

Index

Answer Key

CHAPTER 12: NOUN CLAUSES

PRACTICE 1, p. 108

<u>The fact that Patrick is retiring soon</u> is not a secret. He has been teaching English at the community college for 35 years. He'll miss his students, but he's excited about his retirement. He's especially excited <u>that he'll be able to travel more often</u>. He told me <u>that he's going to Greece this summer</u>. I wonder <u>what other countries he'll visit</u>. I think <u>that his wife is retiring soon too</u>. We're having a retirement dinner for Patrick at his favorite restaurant next month. Everyone is invited to the dinner.

PRACTICE 2, p. 108

1. what he said
2. (none)
3. what happened
4. (none)
5. why Dora is calling me
6. who that man is
7. where Hank lives
8. (none)
9. What they are doing
10. (none)
11. what I should say
12. (none)

PRACTICE 3, p. 108

1. do they want
2. what they want
3. does Stacy live
4. where Stacy lives
5. what Carl likes
6. does Carl like
7. is Lina going
8. where Lina is going

PRACTICE 4, p. 109

1. Where does Lee live? **D**oes he live downtown?
2. I don't know <u>where he lives</u>.
3. What does Sandra want? **D**o you know?
4. Do you know <u>what Sandra wants</u>?
5. <u>What Yoko knows</u> is important to us.
6. We talked about <u>what Yoko knows</u>.
7. What do you think? **D**id you tell your professor <u>what you think</u>?
8. My professor knows <u>what I think</u>.
9. Where is the bus stop? **D**o you know <u>where the bus stop is</u>?
10. What did he report? <u>What he reported</u> is important.

PRACTICE 5, p. 109

1. how far it is
2. what that is on the table
3. how much it cost
4. What he said
5. when they are leaving
6. which road we should take
7. who called
8. what's happening
9. why they work at night
10. What they are trying to do
11. what kind of insects these are
12. whose keys these are

PRACTICE 6, p. 110

1. Who is that man?
   Noun clause: who that man is.
2. Where does George live?
   Noun clause: where George lives.
3. What did Ann buy?
   Noun clause: what Ann bought?
4. How far is it to Denver from here?
   Noun clause: how far it is to Denver from here.
5. Why was Jack late for class?
   Noun clause: why Jack was late for class.
6. Whose pen is that?
   Noun clause: whose pen that is.
7. Who did Alex see at the meeting?
   Noun clause: who Alex saw at the meeting.
8. Who saw Ms. Frost at the meeting?
   Noun clause: who saw Ms. Frost at the meeting?
9. Which book does Alice like best?
   Noun clause: which book Alice likes best.
10. What time is the plane supposed to land?
    Noun clause: what time the plane is supposed to land?

PRACTICE 7, p. 111

1. b	3. e	5. f	7. g, h
2. c	4. a	6. d	

PRACTICE 8, p. 111

1. a, b, c, d, f
2. a, b
3. b, e

PRACTICE 9, p. 112

1. Do you know how much this book costs?
2. Do you know when Flight 62 is expected?
3. Do you know where the nearest restroom is?
4. Do you know if this word is spelled correctly?
5. Do you know what time it is?
6. Do you know if this information is correct?
7. Do you know how much it costs to fly from Toronto to London?
8. Do you know where the bus station is?
9. Do you know whose glasses these are?
10. Do you know if this bus goes downtown?

PRACTICE 10, p. 112

1. d	3. c	5. e	7. h
2. a	4. b	6. g	8. f

PRACTICE 11, p. 112

1. proud
2. angry
3. disappointed
4. aware
5. lucky
6. confident
7. worried ... relieved

PRACTICE 12, p. 113

1. a. is surprising
   b. nobody stopped to help Sam ... is surprising
2. a. is unfortunate that ... .
   b. people in modern cities are ... is unfortunate
3. a. is still true that people ... .
   b. people in my hometown ... help ... is still true.
4. a. is undeniably true that ...
   b. people need each other ... is undeniably true
5. a. seems strange to ... that people in cities often don't know their neighbors
   b. people in cities don't know their neighbors is strange to me

PRACTICE 13, p. 113

1. Millie said, "There's an important meeting at three o'clock."
2. "There's an important meeting at three o'clock," she said.
3. "There is," said Millie, "an important meeting at three o'clock."
4. "There is an important meeting today. It's about the new rules," said Millie.
5. "Where is the meeting?" Carl asked.
6. Robert replied, "It's in the conference room."
7. "How long will it last?" asked Ali.
8. "I don't know how long it will last," replied Millie.
9. "I'll be a little late," said Robert. "I have another meeting until 3:00 P.M. today."
10. "Who is speaking at the meeting?" asked Robert.
11. "I am not sure who is speaking," said Millie, "but you'd better be there. Everybody is supposed to be there."

PRACTICE 14, p. 114

1. was
2. needed
3. was having
4. had finished
5. had finished
6. to stay

PRACTICE 15, p. 114

1. if / whether she was planning
2. what time the movie begins
3. where she had been
4. what Kim's native language is
5. if / whether I was doing
6. why I hadn't called
7. if / whether we had been studying for the test
8. if / whether she had found her phone.

PRACTICE 16, p. 114

1. would arrive
2. was going to be
3. could solve
4. might come
5. might come
6. had to leave
7. had to leave
8. should go

PRACTICE 17, p. 115

1. if we could still get
2. how he could help
3. if / whether he could help
4. when the final decision would be made
5. what time he had
6. who she should give this message
7. where he / she might find
8. how long he / she had to wait
9. when we were going to get

PRACTICE 18, p. 115

Conversation 1

was going ... was ... asked ... would like ... had ... had ... was ... could ... were

Conversation 2

asked ... was ... told ... was ... said ... was ... had heard ... had ... was ... had been ... asked ... had been ... had not ... told ... had gone ... was

PRACTICE 19, p. 116

1. arrive
2. provide
3. get
4. be
5. apply
6. look

PRACTICE 20, p. 117

Part I.

get ... steps Sherri takes ... she gets ... her heart rate is ... whether ... whether or not

Part II.

"Can you help me find a fitness tracker?" Sherri asked.

Mark replied, "Absolutely! What features are you looking for?"

"I'm not sure," Sherri said. "Can you tell me what is available?"

"Sure," Mark answered. "The basic trackers count your steps and monitor your sleep. We also have more sophisticated models if you're looking for a heart rate monitor."

"I can't decide. I think I need to take a look at them," she said.

"Come this way, and I'll show you what we have."

CHAPTER 13: ADJECTIVE CLAUSES

PRACTICE 1, p. 118

When students begin their university studies, they often feel overwhelmed. Most college campuses have several places where students can seek help. The first place that a new student should look for is the advising office. An academic advisor is someone who answers questions that are related to course selection, degree plans, and academic progress. Students usually meet with the same advisor over the course of their university education. The student and advisor develop a relationship in which the advisor serves as a mentor or guide. Another helpful place that students can turn to is the counseling office. A counselor is someone who helps students with personal issues that may or may not be related to the student's academic life. Counselors help students who have trouble with time management, test anxiety, career selection, or similar issues. Both advisors and counselors play an important role in student success.

PRACTICE 2, p. 118

1. person   who fixes computers
2. man   who lives on a boat
3. woman   who speaks four languages
4. people   who are bilingual in the office
5. office   that is in an old building
6. building   that we work in
7. trees   that were over 200 years old
8. trees   which were nearby
9. truck   that had broken down
10. truck   which caused the problem

PRACTICE 3, p. 118

1. a, b
2. a, b
3. c, d
4. a, b
5. b, c
6. b, c

PRACTICE 4, p. 119

1. man   that I met last night
2. woman   that Sandro is going to marry
3. people   whom we invited
4. book   which I just read
5. program   that Jason installed
6. house   we built in 1987
7. cake   I left on the table
8. book   my professor wrote

PRACTICE 5, p. 119

1. a, b, c, f
2. a, c, e, f
3. c, d, e
4. a, b, c, e
5. a, c, d, e
6. a, b, c, f

PRACTICE 6, p. 119

1. … I read was good
2. … I saw was very sad
3. … can live a long time
4. … we photographed
5. … does many things at the same time
6. … can trust
7. … the thieves stole was valuable

PRACTICE 7, p. 120

1. c, d, g, i
2. a, b, f, h

PRACTICE 8, p. 120

1. that / who / whom / Ø
2. who / that
3. that / which / Ø
4. which
5. that / who / whom / Ø
6. who / that
7. whom
8. that / which

PRACTICE 9, p. 121

1. That's a subject I don't want to talk **about**.
2. A person **who writes** with his left hand is called a lefty.
3. Our family brought home a new kitten that we **found at** the animal shelter.
4. What is the name of the podcast **to which** we listened last night? / What is the name of the podcast **that** we listened **to** last night?
5. The candidate for **whom** you vote should be honest.
6. Here's a picture of Nancy **that / which** I took with my phone
7. People **who** have high cholesterol should watch their diets.
8. Suzie is going to marry the man she has always **loved**.
9. There's an article in today's newspaper about a woman **that is** 7 feet tall.
10. Passengers **who / that** have children may board the plane first.

PRACTICE 10, p. 121

1. a. b
   b. a
   c. b
2. a. a
   b. b
3. a. b
   b. a
4. a. a
   b. b

PRACTICE 11, p. 122

1. Do you know the man **whose car** is parked over there?
2. I know a skin doctor **whose name** is Dr. Skinner.
3. The people **whose home** we visited were very hospitable.
4. Mrs. Lake is the teacher **whose class** I enjoy the most.
5. The teacher asked the parents **whose children** were failing to confer with her.

PRACTICE 12, p. 122

1. b, c
2. a, c
3. c
4. a, c
5. a, b
6. b
7. a, c

PRACTICE 13, p. 123

1. a. where I grew up   b. in which I grew up
2. a. which I lived in   b. where I lived
3. a. where I lived   b. on which I lived
4. a. where I played   b. in which I played

PRACTICE 14, p. 123

1. a. that I go
   b. on which I go
   c. when I go
2. a. when I play tennis
   b. that I play tennis
   c. on which I play tennis

PRACTICE 15, p. 124

1. e
2. c
3. f
4. d
5. a
6. h
7. g
8. b

PRACTICE 16, p. 124

1. a, d
2. b
3. c, d
4. a, b, c
5. d
6. b, c
7. c, d
8. a

PRACTICE 17, p. 125

1. d
2. e
3. a
4. c
5. b

PRACTICE 18, p. 125

1. no comma
2. I made an appointment with Dr. Raven, who is …
3. Bogotá, which is the capital of Colombia, is a …
4. no comma
5. South Beach, which is clean, pleasant, and fun, …
6. no comma
7. … Miranda Jones, who wrote ….
8. … Nairobi, which is near several fascinating …
9. no comma
10. no comma
11. no comma
12. no comma
13. A typhoon, which is a violent tropical storm, …
14. no comma
15. Typhoon Haiyan, which destroyed parts of Southeast Asia, occurred in 2013.

PRACTICE 19, p. 125

1. a
2. b
3. a
4. b
5. b
6. a
7. b
8. a

PRACTICE 20, p. 126

1. I received two job offers, neither of which I accepted.
2. I have three brothers, two of whom are professional athletes.
3. Jerry is engaged in several business ventures, only one of which is profitable.
4. The two women, both of whom began their studies at age 40, have almost completed law school.
5. Eric is proud of his success, much of which has been due to hard work, but some of which has been due to good luck.
6. We ordered an extra-large pizza, half of which contained meat and half of which didn't.
7. The scientist won the Nobel Prize for his groundbreaking work, most of which was on genomes.
8. The audience gave a tremendous ovation to the Nobel prize winners, most of whom were scientists.

PRACTICE 21, p. 127

1. Mike was accepted at the state university, which is surprising.
2. Mike did not do well in high school, which is unfortunate.
3. The university accepts a few students each year with a low grade-point average, which is lucky for Mike.
4. The university hopes to motivate these low-performing students, which is a fine idea.
5. Mike might actually be a college graduate one day, which would be wonderful!

PRACTICE 22, p. 127

1. ~~who is wearing a green hat~~ wearing a green hat
2. ~~who is in charge of this department~~ in charge of this department

3. ~~which was painted by Picasso~~ painted by Picasso
4. ~~who are doing research~~ doing research
5. ~~which are in progress~~ in progress
6. ~~which are scheduled to begin in September~~ scheduled to begin in September
7. ~~which is the largest city in Canada~~ the largest city in Canada
8. ~~that orbit the sun~~ orbiting the sun
9. ~~which was formerly known as a planet~~ formerly known as a planet
10. ~~which means to "devalue someone or something"~~ meaning to "devalue someone or something"

PRACTICE 23, p. 127

1. Brasilia, officially inaugurated in 1960, is the capital of Brazil.
2. Rio de Janeiro, the second largest city in Brazil, used to be its capital.
3. Two languages, Finnish and Swedish, are spoken in Helsinki, the capital of Finland.
4. In Canada, you see signs, written in both English and French.
5. Libya, a country in North Africa, is a leading producer of oil.
6. Simon Bolivar, a great South American general, led the fight for independence in the nineteenth century.
7. Five South American countries, liberated by Bolivar, are Venezuela, Colombia, Ecuador, Panama, and Peru.
8. We need someone, holding a degree in electrical engineering, to design this project.
9. The project being built in Beijing will be finished next year.
10. A lot of new buildings were constructed in Beijing in 2008, the site of the summer Olympics that year.

PRACTICE 24, p. 128

Sample answers:

1. … a lot of people waiting in …
2. Students who are living on … OR Students living on …
3. … the librarian who sits … OR the librarian sitting …
4. … Anna whose birthday …
5. … Sapporo, which is …
6. Patrick, who is my oldest brother, is married and has one child.
7. The person sitting next to me is someone I've never met.
8. … is a small city located on …
9. … person to whom I wanted …
10. Yermek, who is from Kazakhstan, teaches Russian classes at the college.
11. The people who we met on our trip last May …
12. Dianne Baxter, who used to teach Spanish, has organized …
13. … since I came here, some of whom are from my country.
14. People who can speak English …
15. Grandpa is getting married again, which is a big surprise.

CHAPTER 14: GERUNDS AND INFINITIVES, PART 1

PRACTICE 1, p. 129

<u>Geocaching</u> has become a popular outdoor activity in recent years. A geocache is a small container that someone has hidden outside. Participants use a GPS or a mobile device (to find) or (hide) geocaches. There are millions of geocaches around the world.

Ray and Isabel are looking for a geocache that someone has hidden. GPS coordinates have been posted on a website. Websites suggest <u>leaving</u> clues in addition to the coordinates, so Ray and Isabel are also using the clues.

The geocache contains a logbook for <u>signing</u> and <u>dating</u>. Some participants like (to place) a small trinket or toy in the geocache. After Ray and Isabel find the geocache, they will sign the logbook. Then they need (to place) the geocache back exactly where they found it.

Ray and Isabel enjoy <u>finding</u> these hidden surprises, but they aren't having much luck today. They have been looking for over an hour, but they can't seem (to find) it. Ray wants (to quit) He's tired and hungry. Isabel prefers (to continue) searching. She doesn't like (to give up)

PRACTICE 2, p. 129

1. playing	5. arguing
2. smoking	6. selling
3. driving	7. having
4. paying	8. reading

PRACTICE 3, p. 130

1. to cook	5. to paint
2. to transfer	6. to work
3. to make	7. to arrive
4. to fly	8. to tell

PRACTICE 4, p. 130

1. a	7. a
2. a	8. a
3. b	9. b
4. b	10. a
5. b	11. a
6. b	12. b

PRACTICE 5, p. 131

1. living	6. being
2. to be	7. humming
3. to show	8. exercising
4. making	9. to exercise
5. to be	10. to graduate

PRACTICE 6, p. 131

1. a, c	4. c
2. c	5. a
3. a, c	6. a, c

PRACTICE 7, p. 131

1. to work
2. me to work
3. to work / me to work
4. to work
5. to work / me to work
6. to work
7. to work
8. me to work
9. me to work
10. to work / me to work
11. to work / me to work
12. to work
13. to work / me to work
14. me to work

PRACTICE 8, p. 132

Part I.

1. to stay	6. him to stay
2. to stay	7. to stay
3. him to stay	8. to stay
4. him to stay	9. him to stay
5. staying	10. to stay

Part II.

1. traveling	6. traveling
2. traveling	7. traveling
3. to travel	8. traveling
4. traveling	9. traveling
5. to travel	10. traveling

Part III.

1. working	6. working
2. to work	7. him to work
3. to work	8. to work
4. to work	9. to work
5. to work	10. working

PRACTICE 9, p. 132

1. a. to turn	3. c. speaking
b. meeting	4. a. buying
2. a. to stop	b. to tell
b. seeing	5. a. to learn
3. a. telling	b. to talk
b. to talk	

PRACTICE 10, p. 133

1. b	4. a
2. a	5. b
3. b	

PRACTICE 11, p. 133

1. a, b	6. a, b
2. a	7. a, b
3. a, b	8. b
4. a	9. b
5. a, b	10. a, b

PRACTICE 12, p. 134

1. taking	5. lowering
2. going	6. buying
3. improving	7. drinking
4. flying	8. hearing

PRACTICE 13, p. 134

1. b	6. c
2. b	7. a
3. c	8. c
4. c	9. c
5. a	10. b

PRACTICE 14, p. 134

1. about leaving
2. for being
3. from completing
4. about having
5. of studying
6. for not wanting
7. for washing … drying
8. of stealing
9. to eating … sleeping
10. for lending

PRACTICE 15, p. 135

1. about taking
2. in buying
3. to living
4. for not answering
5. about failing
6. about changing
7. for cleaning
8. from arriving
9. for writing
10. in saving … from wasting

PRACTICE 16, p. 135

Part I.

1. go hiking
2. go sailing
3. go skiing
4. went birdwatching
5. went canoeing

Part II.

6. go dancing
7. go bowling
8. will go sightseeing
9. will go window shopping

PRACTICE 17, p. 136

1. playing
2. lying
3. locating
4. looking
5. doing
6. watching

PRACTICE 18, p. 136

1. It's
2. is
3. is
4. Is it
5. Going
6. It's
7. is
8. to jump
9. To see
10. Is

PRACTICE 19, p. 137

1. camping
2. to operate
3. getting
4. applying
5. to turn
6. sleeping
7. reading
8. to end
9. using … speaking
10. watching
11. running

PRACTICE 20, p. 138

1. It's important **to keep** your mind active.
2. **Watching** TV is not good brain exercise.
3. I prefer **spending** time **playing** board games and computer games.
4. There is some evidence that older people can avoid **becoming** senile by **exercising** their brain.
5. Playing word **games is** one good way to stimulate your brain.
6. In addition, **it** is beneficial for everyone to exercise regularly.
7. Physical exercise helps the brain by **increasing** the flow of blood and **delivering** more oxygen to the brain.
8. Some studies show that **eating** any type of fish just once a week increases brain health.
9. Doctors advise older people **to eat** fish two or three times a week.
10. Everyone should try **to keep** a healthy brain.

PRACTICE 21, p. 138

1. Pedro is interested **in learning** about other cultures.
2. He has always wanted **to study** abroad.
3. He had difficulty **deciding** where to study.
4. He has finally decided **to live** in Japan next year.
5. He's excited about **attending** a university there.
6. Right now he is struggling **to learn** Japanese.
7. He has a hard time **pronouncing** the words.
8. He keeps on **studying and practicing**.
9. At night, he lies in bed **listening** to Japanese language-teaching programs.
10. The he dreams **about / of traveling** to Japan.

CHAPTER 15: GERUNDS AND INFINITIVES, PART 2

PRACTICE 1, p. 139

to be … to remove, to be removed … placing … loosen up … cleaning, to be cleaned … to scrub … Running … to manage, manage

PRACTICE 2, p. 139

1. a
3. a, b
3. a, b
4. a, b
5. a
6. a
7. a, b
8. a, b
9. a, b
10. a

PRACTICE 3, p. 140

1. to
2. for
3. for
4. for
5. to
6. to
7. for
8. to
9. for

PRACTICE 4, p. 140

1. d
2. c
3. b
4. a
5. f
6. e

PRACTICE 5, p. 140

1. too
2. enough
3. too
4. too
5. too
6. enough
7. too
8. enough
9. enough
10. too
11. too
12. enough
13. too
14. enough
15. too ... enough
16. too ... enough

PRACTICE 6, p. 141

1. a
2. a, b
3. b
4. a

PRACTICE 7, p. 141

1. to be accepted
2. to be given
3. to be picked
4. being petted
5. to be held
6. being asked
7. being noticed
8. being invited
9. to be finished
10. to be submitted

PRACTICE 8, p. 142

1. b
2. a
3. b
4. b
5. a
6. b
7. a
8. b

PRACTICE 9, p. 142

1. b
2. a
3. b
4. b
5. a
6. b
7. b
8. a

PRACTICE 10, p. 143

1. to be called
2. being called
3. to call
4. to be elected
5. to be elected
6. being reelected
7. to elect
8. being understood
9. to understand
10. trying
11. to be left

PRACTICE 11, p. 143

1. a
2. c
3. b, c
4. b, c
5. b, d
6. c, d
7. a, b
8. a, c
9. c, d

PRACTICE 12, p. 144

1. a, c, d
2. a, c, d
3. a, b, c
4. a, b, d
5. a, c
6. b, c

PRACTICE 13, p. 145

1. practice / practicing
2. pass / passing
3. cry / crying
4. leave
5. win
6. arrive
7. rocking / rock
8. doing / do
9. talking / talk
10. reaching / reach

PRACTICE 14, p. 145

1. a
2. b
3. c
4. a, b
5. c
6. a
7. a, c
8. a

PRACTICE 15, p. 146

1. stand
2. fixed
3. beat
4. to stop
5. to clean
6. look
7. call
8. made ... put

PRACTICE 16, p. 146

1. b
2. c
3. b
4. a
5. c
6. b, c
7. b
8. a

PRACTICE 17, p. 146

1. a. your
   b. you
2. a. his
   b. him
3. a. her
   b. her
4. a. their
   b. them
5. a. my
   b. me
6. a. our
   b. us

PRACTICE 18, p. 147

1. b
2. a
3. b
4. c
5. c
6. d
7. d
8. b
9. a
10. b
11. a
12. c
13. d
14. a
15. d
16. a
17. b
18. d

PRACTICE 19, p. 148

1. to buy
2. opening
3. being asked
4. having
5. to wear ... dressing
6. jumping ... falling
7. being taken
8. to stop delivering ... to fill
9. gazing ... to cheer
10. having

PRACTICE 20, p. 149

1. b
2. b
3. b
4. b
5. a
6. b
7. a
8. a
9. a
10. b
11. b
12. a
13. c
14. a
15. b
16. a
17. b
18. c
19. a
20. a
21. c
22. c
23. b
24. a
25. c

PRACTICE 21, p. 150

1. You shouldn't let children **play** with matches.
2. Maddie was lying in bed **crying**.
3. You can get there more quickly by **taking** River Road instead of the interstate highway.
4. Nathan expected **to be** admitted to the university, but he wasn't.
5. Our lawyer advised us not **to sign** the contract until she had a chance to study it very carefully.
6. John was responsible for **notifying** everyone about the meeting.
7. Apparently, he failed to **call** several people.
8. I couldn't understand what the reading said, so I asked my friend **to translate** it for me.
9. You can find out the meaning of the word by **looking** it up in a dictionary.
10. ... How can I make you **understand**?
11. Serena wore a large hat **to** protect her face from the sun.
12. We like to go **fishing** on weekends.
13. Maybe you can get Charlie **to take** you to the airport.
14. My doctor advised me not **to eat** food with a high fat content.
15. Doctors always advise **eating** less and exercising more.
16. Allen smelled something **burning**. ...
17. The player appeared to have been **injured** during the basketball game.
18. David mentioned **having traveled** to China last year.

CHAPTER 16: COORDINATING CONJUNCTIONS

PRACTICE 1, p. 151

1. thyme ... basil ... mint ... oregano
2. seasoning ... brewing ... making
3. herb ... vegetable ... flower
4. space ... knowledge
5. vegetables ... herbs ... hobby ... community ... connection

PRACTICE 2, p. 152

1. b	5. c
2. c	6. c
3. c	7. a
4. b	8. b

PRACTICE 3, p. 152

1. Conjunction: and
   sweet and fresh — a. adjective
2. Conjunction: and
   apples and pears — b. noun
3. Conjunction: and
   washed and dried — c. verb
4. Conjunction: and
   washing and drying — c. verb
5. Conjunction: and
   happily and quickly — d. adverb
6. Conjunction: but
   delicious but expensive — a. adjective
7. Conjunction: and
   Apples, pears, and bananas — b. noun
8. Conjunction: or
   apple or a banana — b. noun
9. Conjunction: and
   red, ripe, and juicy — a. adjective

PRACTICE 4, p. 153

1. c	5. f
2. e	6. d
3. a	7. h
4. g	8. b

PRACTICE 5, p. 153

1. (*none*)
2. ... calm, quiet, and serene
3. ... the ball, and they ran
4. ... kicking, passing, and running
5. ... rocks and insects, had a picnic, and flew kites
6. ... put their phones away, open their reading books, and review their notes
7. (*none*)
8. (*none*)
9. ... two cups of coffee, three glasses of water, one glass of orange juice, and three orders of eggs
10. (*none*)

PRACTICE 6, p. 154

1. I he is honest, and honesty
2. C
3. I quiet quietly
4. C
5. C
6. I to tour touring
7. C
8. I summarizing summarize
9. C
10. C
11. I they require
12. C

PRACTICE 7, p. 154

1. ... stopped. **The** winds ...
2. ... stopped, and the winds ...
3. ... stopped, ... died down, ...
4. ... street. **His** mother ...
5. ... street, and his mother ...
6. ... street. **His** mother ...
7. ... coffee, and ...
8. ... coffee. It is ...
9. ... ice cream, but ... .

PRACTICE 8, p. 154

1. Sherri's graduation was last week, **and now** she's looking for a job.
2. She completed her degree in nursing, **and she** also has a certificate in radiology. OR:
   She completed her degree in **nursing and also** has a certificate in radiology.
3. Sherri doesn't have any full-time work experience, **but she** completed a one-year internship at the hospital.
4. There is a job opening at Lakeside Hospital, **but it** requires five years of nursing experience.

PRACTICE 9, p. 155

1. My brother is visiting me for a couple of days. **We** spent yesterday together in the city, and we had a really good time.
2. **F**irst I took him to the waterfront. **W**e went to the aquarium. **W**e saw fearsome sharks, some wonderfully funny marine mammals, and all kinds of tropical fish. **A**fter the aquarium, we went downtown to a big mall and went shopping.
3. I had trouble thinking of a place to take him for lunch because he's a strict vegetarian, but I remembered a restaurant that has vegan food. **W**e went there, and we had a wonderful lunch of fresh vegetables and whole grains. I'm not a vegetarian, but I must say that I really enjoyed the meal.
4. In the afternoon it started raining. **W**e decided to go to a movie. **I**t was pretty good but had too much violence for me. I felt tense when we left the theater. I prefer comedies or dramas. **M**y brother loved the movie.
5. We ended the day with a delicious home-cooked meal and some good conversation in my living room. **I**t was an excellent day. I like spending time with my brother.

PRACTICE 10, p. 155

1. knows
2. know
3. knows
4. know
5. know
6. wants
7. like
8. has
9. agrees
10. are
11. realizes
12. are

PRACTICE 11, p. 156

1. a. Both Mary and her parents drink coffee.
   b. Neither Mary nor her parents drink coffee.
2. a. Either John or Henry will do the work.
   b. Neither John nor Henry will do the work.
3. a. Our school recycles not only trash but also old electronics.
   b. Our school recycles both trash and old electronics.

PRACTICE 12, p. 156

Part I.
1. I know both her mother and her father.
2. both the nurses and the doctor arrive
3. both bananas and mangos originated
4. both whales and dolphins are

Part II.
5. exports not only coffee but also oil
6. Not only Air Greenland but also Icelandair fly
7. not only a lime-green jacket but also lime-green pants
8. not only attended Harvard University but also Harvard Law School.

Part III.
9. Either Ricky or Paula knows
10. either to Mexico or Costa Rica
11. Either Jim or Taka's parents will take her
12. either salmon or tuna

Part IV.
13. neither Fred nor his children
14. neither she nor her children have
15. Luis has neither a family nor friends
16. neither hot nor cold

PRACTICE 13, p. 157

1. John will call either Mary or Bob.
2. Sue saw not only the mouse but also the cat.
3. Both my mother and father talked to the teacher.
4. Either Mr. Anderson or Ms. Wiggins is going to teach our class today.
5. I enjoy reading not only novels but also magazines.
6. Both smallpox and malaria are dangerous diseases.
7. She wants to buy a compact car. She is saving her money.
8. … snow tonight. The roads …
9. … we attended an opera, … ate at marvelous restaurants, and visited …

PRACTICE 14, p. 158

Across	Down
3. but	1. Neither
4. only	2. Both
6. either	3. and
7. nor	

CHAPTER 17: ADVERB CLAUSES

PRACTICE 1, p. 159

1. Before, As, Whenever, as long as
2. Now that, because
3. While, Even though
4. Whether or not, even if

PRACTICE 2, p. 159

1. as she was leaving the store
2. before we have breakfast
3. Since Douglas fell off his bike last week
4. Because I already had my boarding pass
5. if the workplace is made pleasant
6. After Ceylon had been independent for 24 years
7. as soon as she receives them
8. once he becomes familiar with the new computer program

PRACTICE 3, p. 160

1. … calm. Tom …
2. … calm, Tom …
3. … calm. He …
4. … fishing, the lake was calm. He …
5. … calm, so Tom went fishing. He …
6. … quiet, Tom …
7. … calm, quiet, and clear …
8. … poor, he …
9. … poor. He …
10. Microscopes, automobile dashboards, and cameras … people to use. They are designed … people. When "lefties" use these items, …

PRACTICE 4, p. 160

1. b
2. c
3. d
4. c
5. c
6. d
7. b
8. c
9. b
10. a
11. d
12. a

PRACTICE 5, p. 161

1. 1, 2	5. 2, 1
2. 2, 1	6. 1, 2
3. 1, 2	7. S
4. 2, 1	8. 1, 2

PRACTICE 6, p. 162

1. d	6. j
2. i	7. c
3. a	8. f
4. e	9. b
5. h	10. g

PRACTICE 7, p. 162

1. My registration was cancelled because I didn't pay the registration fee on time.
2. I'm late because there was lot of traffic.
3. Because Harry was on a strict weight-loss diet, he lost 35 pounds.
4. Since Mario's is closed on Sundays, we can't have lunch there tomorrow.
5. Now that Jack has a car, he drives to work.
6. Natalie should find another job since she is very unhappy in this job.
7. David will lead us because he knows the way.
8. Frank is looking for a job in a law office now that he has graduated from law school.

PRACTICE 8, p. 163

1. even though	5. Because
2. because	6. Even though
3. Because	7. even though
4. Even though	8. because

PRACTICE 9, p. 163

1. a. even though
   b. because
2. a. Because
   b. Even though
3. a. even though
   b. because
4. a. because
   b. even though

PRACTICE 10, p. 163

1. c	5. a
2. a	6. c
3. b	7. b
4. b	8. a

PRACTICE 11, p. 164

1. We won't go to the beach if it **rains** tomorrow.
2. If my car doesn't start tomorrow morning, I'll take the bus to work. *(no change)*
3. If I have any free time during my workday, I'll call you.
4. I'll text you if my phone **doesn't** die.
5. If we don't leave within the next ten minutes, we **will be** late for the theater.
6. If **we leave** within the next ten minutes, we will make it to the theater on time.
7. The population of the world will be 9.1 billion in 2050 if it **continues** to grow at the present rate.

PRACTICE 12, p. 165

1. a. so   b. does
   Meaning: If Asraf lives near you
2. a. so   b. are
   Meaning: If you are a resident of Springfield
3. a. not   b. don't
   Meaning: If you don't have enough money
4. a. so   b. are
   Meaning: If you are going to do the laundry
5. a. so   b. did
   Meaning: If I left the water running in the sink

PRACTICE 13, p. 165

1. don't approve ... approve
2. can afford ... can't afford
3. is raining ... isn't raining
4. don't understand ... understand
5. don't want to ... whether you want to

PRACTICE 14, p. 166

1. e	5. c
2. f	6. d
3. a	7. h
4. b	8. g

PRACTICE 15, p. 166

1. unless you can stand the heat
2. unless it is broken
3. unless you cooperate with your opponents
4. unless you help me
5. unless you stop digging

PRACTICE 16, p. 167

1. he wants something
2. she runs out of clean clothes
3. the temperature outside goes below 50 degrees F
4. it is absolutely necessary to get somewhere quickly
5. will you get into Halley College
6. could I afford a big house like that

PRACTICE 17, p. 167

1. pass	7. even if
2. not going to go	8. whether
3. rains	9. won't
4. in case	10. don't wake
5. only if	11. if
6. always eat	12. can we

PRACTICE 18, p. 168

1. h	5. b
2. g	6. d
3. a	7. e
4. f	8. c

PRACTICE 19, p. 168

1. b	6. c
2. b	7. d
3. d	8. b
4. a	9. c
5. b	10. a

CHAPTER 18: REDUCTION OF ADVERB CLAUSES TO MODIFYING ADVERBIAL PHRASES

PRACTICE 1, p. 170

Coloring books for children have always been popular, but lately many adults have been buying coloring books for themselves. It's not unusual these days to see an adult coloring pages <u>while waiting for a doctor's appointment or sitting on a bus</u>. <u>Looking for an easy activity to relieve stress</u>, some people turn to coloring. Research has shown that anxiety levels drop <u>when people color</u>. Coloring is similar to meditation <u>because it helps people focus on the moment</u> <u>while allowing the brain to switch off other thoughts or worries</u>. Other people enjoy coloring <u>because they feel that they can be creative</u> <u>even if they don't have the artistic ability to draw something from scratch</u>. Still others are looking for an escape from technology. <u>Constantly staring at screens all day</u>, adults need a chance to "unplug." Nostalgia is yet another reason for the sudden popularity of adult coloring books. <u>Wanting to feel like a kid again</u>, an adult might open up a coloring book. <u>Since becoming a trend</u>, adult coloring books have become widely available. They can be found in almost any bookstore and have even been included on bestsellers' lists.

PRACTICE 2, p. 170

Grammatically correct items:
2, 3, 4, 6, 8, 10

PRACTICE 3, p. 171

1. he opened	opening
2. I left	leaving
3. I had met	meeting / having met
4. I searched	searching
5. he was herding	herding
6. they marched	marching
7. she was flying	flying
8. they imported	importing

PRACTICE 4, p. 171

1. a. leaving
   b. left
2. a. invented / had invented
   b. inventing / having invented
3. a. working
   b. was working
4. a. flies
   b. flying
5. a. studied
   b. studying
6. a. learning
   b. learned
7. a. taking
   b. take
8. a. was driving
   b. driving

PRACTICE 5, p. 172

Subjects
1. (no change)
2. While driving to work, Sam had a flat tire.
3. Adv. clause: Nick; Main clause: son (no change)
4. Adv. clause: Nick; Main clause: he
   Before leaving on his trip, Nick gave his itinerary to his secretary.
5. Adv. clause: Tom; Main clause: he
   After working in the garden all afternoon, Tom took a shower and then …
6. Adv. clause: Sunita; Main clause: they (no change)
7. Adv. clause: she; Main clause: Emily
   Emily always clears off her desk before leaving the office at the end of the day.

PRACTICE 6, p. 172

Modifying Adverbial Phrases

1. Riding his bicycle to school	a
2. Being seven feet tall	b
3. Driving to work this morning	a
4. Running five miles on a very hot day	a, b
5. Having run for 26 miles in the marathon	b
6. Drinking a tall glass of refreshing iced tea	a, b
7. Clapping loudly at the end of the game	a
8. Speaking with her guidance counselor	a
9. Knowing that I was going to miss the plane because of heavy traffic	b
10. Having missed my plane	b
11. Waiting for my plane to depart	a

PRACTICE 7, p. 173

1. h	6. a
2. i	7. c
3. j	8. f
4. b	9. e
5. d	10. g

PRACTICE 8, p. 173

1. b, c	5. a, c
2. a, b, c	6. b, c
3. a, b	7. a, c
4. a, b	

PRACTICE 9, p. 174

1. a. Upon receiving her acceptance letter for medical school, Sarah …
   b. On receiving her acceptance letter for medical school, Sarah …
2. a. Upon hearing the sad news, Kathleen …
   b. When she heard the sad news, Kathleen …
3. a. On looking at the accident victim, the paramedics …
   b. When they looked at the accident victim, the paramedics …

PRACTICE 10, p. 174

2. e. reaching the other side of the lake
3. c. discovering a burned-out wire
4. a. learning that the problem was not at all serious
5. b. being told she got it

PRACTICE 11, p. 175

1. d	6. h
2. a	7. g
3. f	8. b
4. i	9. e
5. j	10. c

PRACTICE 12, p. 175
1. (no change)
2. After finishing something very easy
3. (no change)
4. When doing or saying something exactly right
5. While working late in the night
6. After waking up in a bad mood
7. Having lost all my work when my computer crashed
8. (no change)

CHAPTER 19: CONNECTIVES THAT EXPRESS CAUSE AND EFFECT, CONTRAST, AND CONDITION

PRACTICE 1, p. 176
Parents often buy noisy electronic toys for their babies <u>because</u> these toys seem educational. <u>If</u> a toy talks or plays music, many parents believe that the toy is teaching the sounds and structure of language. <u>However,</u> some researchers believe electronic toys actually delay language development in small children. They believe this happens <u>due to</u> a lack of human interaction. <u>Because of</u> their busy schedules, parents often buy electronic toys to keep their children occupied. <u>Consequently,</u> these parents might spend less time talking to and interacting with their children. <u>While</u> electronic toys are entertaining, the most important skill for babies to learn is how to communicate with other people. <u>Even if</u> electronic toys sing the alphabet or say the names of shapes and colors, they do not promote communication. <u>On the other hand,</u> more traditional toys such as puzzles and blocks seem to encourage babies to communicate. Studies have found that books produce the most communication between parents and babies. <u>Whether or not</u> parents buy electronic toys, they should try to interact with their babies as much as possible.
1. because, due to, because of, consequently
2. however, while, on the other hand
3. if, even if, whether or not

PRACTICE 2, p. 176
1. b, c, f
2. a, d, e
3. a, c, e
4. b, d, f

PRACTICE 3, p. 177
1. because
2. because
3. due to / because of
4. because
5. due to / because of
6. because
7. because
8. due to / because of

PRACTICE 4, p. 177
1. heavy traffic
2. there was heavy traffic
3. he is getting old
4. his age
5. she is afraid of heights
6. her fear of heights
7. a cancellation
8. there was a cancellation today

PRACTICE 5, p. 177
1. Because she had a headache, she took some aspirin.
2. No change
3. Because of her headache, she took some aspirin.
4. No change
5. She had a headache. **T**herefore, she took some aspirin.
6. She had a headache. **S**he, therefore, took some aspirin.
7. She had a headache. **S**he took some aspirin, therefore.
8. She had a headache, so she took some aspirin.

PRACTICE 6, p. 178
Sentence 1
1. a
2. b
3. c

Sentence 2
1. a
2. b
3. a
4. b

PRACTICE 7, p. 178
1. b. Because the store didn't have any orange juice, I bought lemonade
   c. The store didn't have any orange juice. Therefore, I bought lemonade.
   d. The store didn't have any orange juice, so I bought lemonade.
2. a. Max has excellent grades. Therefore, he will go to a top university.
   b. Max has excellent grades. He, therefore, will go to a top university.
   c. Max has excellent grades. He will go to a top university, therefore.
   d. Max has excellent grades, so he will go to a top university.
3. a. Because there had been no rain for several months, the crops died.
   b. There had been no rain for several months. Consequently, the crops died.
   c. There had been no rain for several months. The crops, therefore, died.
   d. There had been no rain for several months, so the crops died.

PRACTICE 8, p. 179
Part I.
1. Because
2. Therefore,
3. because of
4. Therefore,
5. Therefore,
6. because of
7. Because
8. Because of

Part II.
9. Due to his poor eyesight, John
10. Since John has poor eyesight,
11. ... poor eyesight. Consequently,
12. ... heights. Consequently,
13. due to
14. ... overweight. Consequently,
15. Since

PRACTICE 9, p. 179

3. Edward missed the final exam. **H**e simply forgot to go to it.
4. Because we forgot to make a reservation, we couldn't get a table at our favorite restaurant last night.
5. The server kept coming to work late or not at all. **T**herefore, she was fired.
6. The server kept forgetting customers' orders, so he was fired.
7. No change
8. The needle has been around since prehistoric times. **T**he button was invented about 2,000 years ago. **T**he zipper wasn't invented until 1890.
9. It is possible for wildlife observers to identify individual zebras because the patterns of stripes on each zebra are unique. **N**o two zebras are alike.
10. When students in the United States are learning to type, they often practice this sentence: *The quick brown fox jumps over the lazy dog* because it contains all the letters of the English alphabet.

PRACTICE 10, p. 180

Sentence 1
a. Because she ate some bad food, Kim got sick.
b. Because of some bad food, Kim got sick.
c. Kim ate some bad food, so she got sick.
d. Due to some bad food, Kim got sick.

Sentence 2
a. Adam had driven for 13 hours. Therefore, he was exhausted.
b. Since Adam had driven for 13 hours, he was exhausted.
c. Due to the fact that Adam had driven for 13 hours, he was exhausted.
d. Adam had driven for 13 hours, so he was exhausted.

PRACTICE 11, p. 180

1. such	6. so
2. so	7. so
3. so	8. such
4. such	9. so
5. such	10. so

PRACTICE 12, p. 180

1. It was such a nice day that we took a walk.
2. Jeff was so late that he missed the meeting.
3. She talked so fast that I couldn't understand her.
4. It was such an expensive car that we couldn't afford to buy it.
5. There were so few people at the meeting that it was canceled.
6. Ted was so worried about the exam that he couldn't fall asleep last night.
7. The tornado struck with such great force that it lifted cars off the ground.
8. Joe's handwriting is so illegible that I can't figure out what this sentence says.
9. David has so many girlfriends that he can't remember all of their names.
10. There were so many people at the meeting that there were not enough seats for everyone.

PRACTICE 13, p. 181
Sentences 1, 3, 4, 5, 7, 8 express purpose

PRACTICE 14, p. 181

1. d	6. c
2. i	7. e
3. a	8. g
4. f	9. h
5. j	10. b

PRACTICE 15, p. 182

1. Rachel turned on the TV so that she could watch the news.
2. Alex wrote down the time and date of his appointment so (that) he wouldn't forget to go.
3. Nancy is taking extra courses every semester so (that) she can graduate early.
4. Amanda turned down the TV so (that) she wouldn't disturb her roommate.
5. Chris took some change from his pocket so (that) he could buy a snack from the vending machine.
6. I turned on the TV so (that) I could listen to the news while I was making dinner.
7. I turned off my phone so (that) I wouldn't be interrupted while I was working.
8. It's a good idea for you to learn keyboarding skills so (that) you'll be able to use your computer more efficiently.
9. Lynn tied a string around her finger so (that) she wouldn't forget to take her book back to the library.
10. Wastebaskets have been placed throughout the park so (that) people won't litter.

PRACTICE 16, p. 182

1. is	6. isn't
2. is	7. is
3. isn't	8. isn't
4. is	9. isn't
5. is	10. is

PRACTICE 17, p. 183

1. a. Even though
   b. Despite
   c. Despite
   d. Despite
   e. Even though
2. a. In spite of
   b. Although
   c. Although
   d. In spite of
   e. In spite of
3. a. Despite
   b. Although
   c. Despite
   d. Although
   e. Despite
4. a. In spite of
   b. Even though
   c. in spite of
   d. even though
   e. in spite of
   f. even though
   g. even though
   h. in spite of

PRACTICE 18, p. 184

1. e	6. i
2. c	7. d
3. b	8. j
4. g	9. h
5. a	10. f

PRACTICE 19, p. 184

1. a. Even though it was night, we could see the road very clearly.
   b. Although it was night, we could see the road very clearly.
   c. It was night, but we could see the road very clearly.
2. a. Despite the fact that Helena has a fear of heights, she enjoys skydiving.
   b. Despite her fear of heights, Helena enjoys skydiving.
   c. Helena has a fear of heights; nevertheless, she enjoys skydiving.
3. a. Though Millie has the flu, she is working at her computer.
   b. Millie has the flu, but she is working at her computer anyway.
   c. Millie has the flu, but she is still working at her computer.

PRACTICE 20, p. 185

Possible answers

1. Red is bright and lively, while gray is a dull color. OR While red is bright and lively, gray is a dull color.
2. Jane is insecure and unsure of herself. **Her sister, on the other hand,** is full of self-confidence.
3. **While** a rock is heavy, a feather is light. OR **A** rock is heavy, **while** a feather is light.
4. **S**ome children are unruly. **O**thers, **however,** are quiet and obedient. OR
   Some children are unruly; others, **however,** are quiet and obedient. OR
   Some children are unruly. **O**thers are quiet and obedient, **however.**
5. **L**anguage and literature classes are easy and enjoyable for Alex. **On the other hand,** math and science courses are difficult for him. OR
   Language and literature classes are easy and enjoyable for Alex; **on the other hand,** math and science courses are difficult for him.
6. **S**trikes can bring improvements in wages and working conditions; **however,** they can also cause loss of jobs and bankruptcy. OR
   Strikes can bring improvements in wages and working conditions. **T**hey can also cause loss of jobs and bankruptcy, **however.**

PRACTICE 21, p. 185

1. I **should / had better / have to** call my mother. **Otherwise,** she'll start worrying about me.
2. The bus **had better** come soon. **Otherwise,** we'll be late for work.
3. You **should / had better / have to** make a reservation. **Otherwise,** you won't get seated at the restaurant.
4. Beth **should / had better / has to** stop complaining. **Otherwise,** she will lose the few friends she has.
5. You **have to / had better** have a government-issued ID. **Otherwise,** you can't get on the plane.
6. Louis **had better / has to** apply for his driver's license in person. **Otherwise,** he can't replace it.
7. You **have to be** a registered voter. **Otherwise,** you can't vote in the general election.
8. You **should** clean up the kitchen tonight. **Otherwise,** you'll have to clean it up early tomorrow.

PRACTICE 22, p. 186

1. e	5. b
2. h	6. f
3. d	7. a
4. g	8. c

PRACTICE 23, p. 186

1. exports	4. is
2. doesn't export	5. originated
3. uses	6. is

PRACTICE 24, p. 187

1. passes	5. doesn't pass
2. doesn't pass	6. passes
3. passes	7. doesn't pass
4. passes	

PRACTICE 25, p. 187

1. the flowers bloomed
2. I took good care of the garden
3. my care
4. my care
5. , the flowers didn't bloom
6. … ; therefore, the flowers didn't bloom
7. ; however, the flowers bloomed
8. … garden. **N**evertheless, the flowers did not bloom
9. … garden, so the flowers did not bloom
10. … garden, the flowers bloomed
11. … garden, the flowers didn't bloom
12. the flowers bloomed anyway
13. … garden, the flowers will bloom
14. … garden, the flowers will not bloom
15. … garden. **O**therwise, the flowers will not bloom
16. … garden. **C**onsequently, the flowers did not bloom
17. … garden. **N**onetheless, the flowers bloomed
18. the flowers will bloom
19. will the flowers bloom
20. , yet the flowers did not bloom
21. the flowers won't bloom
22. or not you take good care of the garden

CHAPTER 20: CONDITIONAL SENTENCES AND WISHES

PRACTICE 1, p. 188

If you have ever been snorkeling or scuba diving, you may have seen a coral reef. Coral reefs look like rocks, but they are actually living creatures. Because reefs are so colorful and are home to such a large number of sea creatures, some people describe them as cities or rain forests of the ocean.

Unfortunately, coral reefs all around the world are dying. If a reef dies, so will a lot of the sea life around the reef. Coral reefs are an important part of the ocean food chain. They also provide shelter for many animals, such as fish, sponges, eels, jellyfish, sea stars, and shrimp. If there were no coral reefs, many species would simply not exist. If these creatures no longer existed, millions of people who depend on fish for their main food supply and livelihood would go hungry.

There are actions we can take to protect coral reefs. Pollution is one of the biggest problems for all sea life. If we choose to walk or bike instead of driving cars, there will be fewer pollutants. Another major problem is overfishing. If governments restrict or limit fishing around reefs, the reefs might have a chance of survival. Most importantly, we need to raise awareness. If more people were aware of the dangers of dying reefs, the reefs would probably not be in such bad condition. With greater awareness, more people will volunteer with beach and reef cleanup and be careful when swimming or diving near fragile reefs. If we follow these actions, we can keep our reefs around for future generations.

PRACTICE 2, p. 188

1. a. yes
   b. no
2. a. yes
   b. no
3. a. no
   b. yes

4. a. no
   b. no
   c. yes
5. a. no
   b. no
   c. yes
   d. no

PRACTICE 3, p. 189

Group 1
1. c
2. a
3. b

Group 2
1. c
2. a
3. b

Group 3
1. c
2. b
3. a

Group 4
1. a
2. c
3. b

PRACTICE 4, p. 189

1. heat ... boils
   heat ... will boil
2. forget ... look
   forget ... will look
3. pet ... purrs
   pet ... will purr

4. have ... will call
   have ... call
5. eat ... won't feel
   eat ... don't feel
6. is ... are
   is ... will be

PRACTICE 5, p. 190

1. b
2. a
3. b

4. a
5. b
6. b

PRACTICE 6, p. 191

1. were ... would be
2. had ... would travel
3. had ... would like
4. liked ... would cook
5. weren't ... could have
6. didn't have ... would go / 'd go

PRACTICE 7, p. 191

1. h
2. d
3. b

4. j
5. i
6. c

7. a
8. e

9. g
10. f

PRACTICE 8, p. 192

1. b
2. a
3. a

4. a
5. b
6. b

PRACTICE 9, p. 192

1. had not taken ... would not have met
2. had not forgotten ... could have paid
3. had known ... would have visited
4. had paid ... would not have cut off
5. had been ... would not have been canceled
6. had not discovered ... would not have developed

PRACTICE 10, p. 192

1. c
2. a
3. b

4. e
5. f
6. d

PRACTICE 11, p. 193

1. had ... could fly
2. could fly ... would get
3. get ... will have / 'll have
4. have ... will tell / 'll tell
5. had had ... would have told him
6. had told ... would not have been

PRACTICE 12, p. 193

1. I hadn't been sick yesterday, I would have gone to class.
2. Alan ate breakfast, he wouldn't overeat at lunch.
3. his watch had not been slow, Kostas would not have been late to his own wedding.
4. the bus were not always so crowded, I would ride it to work every morning.
5. Sara had known that Highway 57 was closed, she would have taken an alternative route.
6. someone had been there to help her, Camille could have finished unloading the truck.

PRACTICE 13, p. 194

1. If the wind weren't blowing so hard, we could go sailing.
2. If the wind had not been blowing so hard, we could have gone sailing.
3. If the water weren't running, I could hear you.
4. If the water had not been running, I could have heard the phone.
5. If the baby were not hungry, she wouldn't be crying.
6. If Jude had not been sleeping soundly, he would have heard his alarm clock.
7. If I had not been watching an exciting mystery on TV, I would have answered the phone.
8. If I weren't trying to concentrate, I could talk to you now.

PRACTICE 14, p. 194

1. a, c
2. b, d
3. a, d

4. b, c
5. a, d
6. a, d

PRACTICE 15, p. 195

1. If it weren't raining, we would finish the game.
2. If I had eaten lunch, I wouldn't be hungry now.
3. If Bob hadn't left his wallet at home, he would have money for lunch now.
4. If Bryce were not always daydreaming, he would get his work done.
5. If I hadn't played basketball for three hours last night, my muscles wouldn't hurt today.
6. If the band had not been playing so loud, I could have heard what you said.
7. If Diana had not asked the technician a lot of questions, she wouldn't understand how to fix her computer now.
8. If Sasha and Ivan had been paying attention, they would have seen the exit sign on the highway.
9. If the doctor had explained the test results to me, I would know what they mean.
10. If we had not been sleeping last night, we would have felt the earthquake.

PRACTICE 16, p. 196

1. Were I you,
2. Should you need
3. Had I known
4. Had I been offered
5. Should anyone call
6. Should the pizza need reheating
7. Should you feel
8. Were you really a lawyer

PRACTICE 17, p. 196

1. b		4. b	
2. b		5. b	
3. c			

PRACTICE 18, p. 197

1. I hadn't forgotten to tell him that she needed a ride
2. you hadn't helped
3. I had opened the door quickly
4. he could have gotten time off from work
5. he had told his boss about the problem

PRACTICE 19, p. 197

1. d	11. c
2. a	12. d
3. c	13. b
4. d	14. d
5. c	15. c
6. d	16. b
7. c	17. b
8. b	18. b
9. b	19. a
10. a	20. c

PRACTICE 20, p. 198

1. b	4. b
2. b	5. b
3. a	6. b

PRACTICE 21, p. 199

1. were shining	5. had won
2. had gone	6. had gotten
3. had driven	7. hadn't quit
4. could swim	8. were

PRACTICE 22, p. 199

1. had gone ... could paint
2. hadn't moved ... had taken
3. would stop
4. hadn't invited
5. hadn't paid
6. A: would hurry
   B: would relax
7. A: hadn't been chosen
   B: had picked
8. A: weren't ... were
   B: were ... were
9. had told
10. would go

PRACTICE 23, p. 200

1. would get	4. would hang up
2. would snow	5. would end
3. would leave	6. would cook

PRACTICE 24, p. 201

1. allowed
2. had gotten
3. had thought
4. didn't have
5. could get
6. could take OR would take

PRACTICE 25, p. 202

1. would look
2. had had
3. hadn't been driving
4. would not have slid
5. steps
6. had known
7. would not have crashed
8. had not lost
9. would have had
10. had had
11. would not have to pay
12. would not have run into
13. would not be
14. were
15. would take
16. stay
17. would stay
18. were not
19. could go
20. will fly
21. will take
22. could drive
23. would be
24. had

APPENDIX: SUPPLEMENTARY GRAMMAR CHARTS

PRACTICE 1, p. 203

1. Airplanes have wings.
   (S V O)
2. The teacher explained the problem.
   (S V O)
3. Children enjoy games.
   (S V O)
4. Jack wore a blue suit.
   (S V O)
5. Some animals eat plants. Some animals eat other animals.
   (S V O S V O)
6. According to an experienced waitress, you can carry full cups of coffee without spilling them just by never looking at them.
   (S V O)

PRACTICE 2, p. 203

1. Alice arrived at six o'clock. (VI)
2. We drank some tea. (VT)
3. I agree with you. (VI)
4. I waited for Sam at the airport for two hours. (VI)
5. They're staying at a resort hotel in San Antonio, Texas. (VI)
6. Mr. Chan is studying English. (VI)
7. The wind is blowing hard today. (VI)
8. I walked to the theater, but Janice rode her bicycle. (VI / VT)
9. Crocodiles hatch from eggs. (VI)
10. Rivers flow toward the sea. (VI)

PRACTICE 3, p. 203

1. Jack opened the heavy door slowly. (ADJ ADV)
2. Chinese jewelers carved beautiful ornaments from jade. (ADJ ADJ)
3. The old man carves wooden figures skillfully. (ADJ ADJ ADV)
4. A busy executive usually has short conversations on the telephone. (ADJ ADV ADJ)
5. The young woman had a very good time at the picnic yesterday. (ADJ ADV ADJ ADV)

PRACTICE 4, p. 204

1. quickly
2. quick
3. polite
4. politely
5. regularly
6. regular
7. usual
8. usually
9. well
10. good
11. gentle
12. gently
13. bad
14. badly

PRACTICE 5, p. 204

1. Ana **always takes** a walk in the morning.
2. Tim **is always** a hard worker.
3. Beth **has always worked** hard.
4. Carrie **always works** hard.
5. **Do you always work** hard?
6. Taxis **are usually** available …
7. Yusef **rarely takes** a taxi … .
8. I **have often thought** about … .
9. Yuko **probably needs** some help.
10. **Have you ever attended** the show … ?
11. Brad **seldom goes** out … .
12. The students **are hardly ever** late.
13. **Do you usually finish** your … ?
14. In India, the monsoon season **generally begins** …
15. … Mr. Singh's hometown **usually receives** around… .

PRACTICE 6, p. 205

1. Jim came to class without his books.
2. We stayed at home during the storm.
3. Sonya walked across the bridge over the Cedar River.
4. When Alex walked through the door, his little sister ran toward him and put her arms around his neck.
5. The two of us need to talk to Tom too.
6. Animals live in all parts of the world. Animals walk or crawl on land, fly in the air, and swim in the water.
7. Scientists divide living things into two main groups: the animal kingdom and the plant kingdom.
8. Asia extends from the Pacific Ocean in the east to Africa and Europe in the west.

PRACTICE 7, p. 205

1. Harry put the letter in the mailbox.
   (S V O PP)
2. The kids walked to school.
   (S V PP)
3. Caroline did her homework at the library.
   (S V O PP)
4. Chinese printers created the first paper money in the world.
   (S V O PP)
5. Dark clouds appeared on the horizon.
   (S V PP)
6. Rhonda filled the shelves of the cabinet with boxes of old books.
   (S V O PP PP PP)

PRACTICE 8, p. 205

1. honesty, fairness
2. school, class
3. her illness, her husband's death
4. jail, prison
5. ghosts, UFOs
6. my cousin, a friend
7. mathematics, sports
8. you, your children
9. smoking, cigarettes
10. magazines, a newspaper, websites

PRACTICE 9, p. 205

1. of
2. at
3. from
4. in
5. at
6. of
7. to
8. for
9. on
10. from

PRACTICE 10, p. 206

Situation 1:
1. to
2. to
3. of
4. to
5. with
6. to
7. to

Situation 2:
1. with / by
2. with
3. with
4. of
5. of
6. of, by

PRACTICE 11, p. 206

1. c
2. e
3. b
4. f
5. a
6. g
7. d

PRACTICE 12, p. 207

1. to
2. for
3. from
4. on
5. about
6. for
7. about
8. with
9. on
10. with
11. on
12. of

PRACTICE 13, p. 207

1. for
2. for
3. of
4. to ... for
5. with
6. to
7. on
8. for ... to
9. about
10. of
11. of
12. to / with
13. with
14. to

PRACTICE 14, p. 208

	Question word	Auxiliary verb	Subject	Main verb	Rest of question
1a.	Ø	Can	Chris	live	there?
1b.	Where	can	Chris	live	Ø?
1c.	Who	can	Ø	live	there?
2a.	Ø	Is	Ron	living	there?
2b.	Where	is	Ron	living	Ø?
2c.	Who	is	Ø	living	there?
3a.	Ø	Does	Kate	live	there?
3b.	Where	does	Kate	live	Ø?
3c.	Who	Ø	Ø	lives	there?
4a.	Ø	Will	Ann	live	there?
4b.	Where	will	Ann	live	Ø?
4c.	Who	will	Ø	live	there?
5a.	Ø	Did	Jack	live	there?
5b.	Where	did	Jack	live	Ø?
5c.	Who	Ø	Ø	lived	there?
6a.	Ø	Has	Mary	lived	there?
6b.	Where	has	Mary	lived	Ø?
6c.	Who	has	Ø	lived	there?

PRACTICE 15, p. 209

1. When are you going to the zoo?
2. Are you going downtown later today?
3. Do you live in an apartment?
4. Where does Alex live?
5. Who lives in that house?
6. Can you speak French?
7. Who can speak Arabic?
8. When did Ben arrive?
9. Who arrived late?
10. What is Ann opening?
11. What is Ann doing?
12. What did Mary open?
13. Who opened the door?
14. Has the mail arrived?
15. Do you have a bicycle?
16. What does Zach have in his hand?
17. Do you like ice cream?
18. Would you like an ice cream cone?
19. What would Scott like?
20. Who would like a soft drink?

PRACTICE 16, p. 210

1. How do you take your coffee?
2. What kind of dictionary do you have? (have you? / have you got?)
3. What does he do for a living?
4. Who was Margaret talking to? / To whom was Margaret talking?
5. How many people showed up for the meeting?
6. Why could none of the planes take off?
7. What was she thinking about? / About what was she thinking?
8. How fast / How many miles per hour (OR: an hour) were you driving when the police officer stopped you?
9. What kind of food do you like best?
10. Which apartment is yours?
11. What is Oscar like? (also possible: What kind of person / man is Oscar?)
12. What does Oscar look like?
13. Whose dictionary fell to the floor?
14. Why isn't Abby here?

15. When will all of the students in the class be informed of their final grades?
16. How do you feel?
17. Which book did you prefer?
18. What kind of music do you like?
19. How late is the plane expected to be?
20. Why did the driver of the stalled car light a flare?
21. Which pen do you want?
22. What's the weather like in July?
23. How do you like your steak?
24. How did you do on the test?
25. How many seconds are there in a year?

PRACTICE 17, p. 211
1. How much money do you need?
2. Where was Roberto born? / In what country / city was ...? / What country / city was Roberto born in?
3. How often do you go out to eat?
4. Who(m) are you waiting for? (very formal and seldom used: For whom are you waiting?)
5. Who answered the phone?
6. Who(m) did you call?
7. Who called?
8. How much gas / How many gallons of gas did she buy?
9. What does *deceitful* mean?
10. What is an abyss?
11. Which way did he go?
12. Whose books and papers are these?
13. How many children do they have? [British or regional American: How many children have they?]
14. How long has he been here?
15. How far is it / How many miles is it to Madrid?
16. When / At what time can the doctor see me?
17. Who is her roommate?
18. Who are her roommates?
19. How long / How many years have your parents been living there?
20. Whose book is this?
21. Who's coming over for dinner?
22. What color is Caroline's dress?
23. What color are Caroline's eyes?
24. Who can't go ... ?
25. Why can't Andrew go? / How come Andrew can't go?
26. Why didn't you / How come you didn't answer ... ? (formal and rare: Why did you not answer the phone?)
27. What kind of music do you like?
28. What don't you understand?
29. What is Janie doing right now?
30. How do you spell sitting? [you = impersonal pronoun]
31. What does Xavier look like?
32. What is Xavier like?
33. What does Ray do (for a living)?
34. How far / How many miles is Mexico from here?
35. How do you take / like your coffee?
36. Which (city) is farther north, Stockholm or Moscow? / Of Stockholm and Moscow, which (city / one) is farther north?
37. How are you getting along?

PRACTICE 18, p. 212
1. Did you find your keys?
2. Do you want some coffee?
3. Do you need help?
4. Are you leaving already?
5. Do you have any questions?
6. Are you going up?
7. Did you make it on time?

PRACTICE 19, p. 212
1. Haven't you seen ... ? No.
2. Don't you feel ... ? No.
3. Wasn't he ... ? No.
4. Didn't Dana tell ... ? No.
5. Don't Jill and you work ... ? Yes.
6. Isn't that ... ? Yes.
7. Wasn't she ... ? No.
8. Isn't she ... ? Yes.

PRACTICE 20, p. 213
1. don't you
2. have you
3. didn't she
4. aren't there
5. have you
6. don't you (also possible but less common: haven't you)
7. won't you
8. doesn't he
9. shouldn't we
10. can they
11. are they
12. isn't it
13. didn't they
14. aren't I
15. isn't it

PRACTICE 21, p. 213
1. He's
2. Ø
3. He's
4. Ø
5. She'd
6. Ø
7. She'd
8. Ø
9. We'll
10. They're
11. It's
12. It's
13. Ø
14. Ø
15. We're
16. Ø
17. She's
18. She'd
19. She'd ... we'd
20. he'd

PRACTICE 22, p. 214
1. I don't have any problems. I have no problems.
2. There wasn't any food on the shelf. There was no food on the shelf.
3. I didn't receive any letters from home. I received no letters from home.
4. I don't need any help. I need no help.
5. We don't have any time to waste. We have no time to waste.
6. You shouldn't have given the beggar any money. You should have given the beggar no money.
7. I don't trust anyone. I trust no one.
8. I didn't see anyone. I saw no one.
9. There wasn't anyone in his room. There was no one in his room.
10. She can't find anybody who knows about it. She can find nobody who knows about it.

PRACTICE 23, p. 214

1. We have no time to waste. or We don't have any time to waste.
2. I didn't have any problems. or I had no problems.
3. I can't do anything about it. or I can do nothing about it.
4. You can hardly ever understand her when she speaks.
5. I know neither Joy nor her husband. or I don't know either Joy or her husband.
6. Don't ever drink water from … . or Never drink water from … .
7. … I could barely hear the speaker.

PRACTICE 24, p. 214

1. Hardly had I stepped out of bed … .
2. Never will I say that again.
3. Scarcely ever have I enjoyed myself more … .
4. Rarely does she make a mistake.
5. Never will I trust him again because … .
6. Hardly ever is it possible to get … .
7. Seldom do I skip breakfast.
8. Never have I known a more … .

PRACTICE 25, p. 215

	Just add -ing	Drop the final -e	Double the final letter
1.		arriving	
2.	copying		
3.			cutting
4.	enjoying		
5.	filling		
6.	happening		
7.		hoping	
8.		leaving	
9.		making	
10.			rubbing
11.	staying		
12.			stopping
13.		taking	
14.			winning
15.	working		

PRACTICE 26, p. 215

	Just add -ed	Add -d only	Double the final letter	Change -y to -i
1.	bothered			
2.				copied
3.	enjoyed			
4.		snored		
5.	feared			
6.			occurred	
7.			patted	
8.	played			
9.	rained			
10.			referred	
11.				replied
12.	returned			
13.		scared		
14.				tried
15.	walked			

PRACTICE 27, p. 216

1. rains
2. visited
3. will win
4. is watching
5. will be flying
6. was thinking
7. will be working
8. went … were sleeping
9. fell … will help
10. are swimming

PRACTICE 28, p. 216

1. have
2. had
3. has been
4. was
5. will have been
6. have lived
7. had
8. have
9. had
10. had

PRACTICE 29, p. 216

1. have
2. has been
3. will have been
4. had
5. have
6. had
7. have been waiting
8. has
9. had

PRACTICE 30, p. 217

1. eats
2. ate
3. will eat / 'll eat
4. am eating / 'm eating
5. was eating
6. will be eating
7. have already eaten
8. had already eaten
9. will have already eaten
10. has been eating
11. had been eating
12. will have been eating

PRACTICE 31, p. 218

	L.VERB	+ ADJ
1.	Ø (no linking verb in the sentence)	
2.	looked	fresh
3.	Ø	
4.	Ø	
5.	tasted	good
6.	grew	quiet
7.	Ø	
8.	Ø	
9.	Ø	
10.	smells	delicious
11.	Ø	
12.	got	sleepy
13.	became	rough
14.	Ø	
15.	Ø	
16.	sounded	happy
17.	turns	hot
18.	Ø	
19.	Ø	
20.	appears	certain
21.	seems	strange

PRACTICE 32, p. 219

1. clean
2. slowly
3. safely
4. anxious
5. complete
6. wildly
7. honest
8. thoughtfully
9. well
10. fair
11. terrible
12. good
13. light
14. confidently
15. famous
16. fine

PRACTICE 33, p. 219

1. raised
2. rises
3. sat
4. set
5. lay
6. lying
7. laid
8. lie

SPECIAL WORKBOOK SECTION: PHRASAL VERBS

PRACTICE 1, p. 223

1. a. after
   b. over
   c. up
   d. into
2. a. out
   b. into
   c. out
   d. out of
3. a. over
   b. through with
   c. out of
   d. back from
   e. off
4. a. off
   b. up
   c. on
   d. back
   e. in

PRACTICE 2, p. 224

1. passed out
2. Pick out
3. takes after
4. think ... over
5. puts up with
6. passed away
7. show up
8. get along with
9. turn in
10. pass out

PRACTICE 3, p. 224

1. our assignment?
2. a lie. / a story.
3. the city. / the banks.
4. your cigarette. / the lights. / the fire.
5. the war? / the crisis?
6. the problem? / the puzzle?
7. the lights? / the music? / the printer?
8. his classmate. / a girl.

9. chocolate. / smoking.
10. a friend. / a classmate.
11. high school. / college.

PRACTICE 4, p. 225

1. into
2. off
3. on
4. back
5. out
6. up
7. into ... out
8. up
9. up
10. on

PRACTICE 5, p. 226

1. away / out
2. up
3. off / out
4. up
5. off
6. up
7. about, on
8. out of
9. off
10. off ... in

PRACTICE 6, p. 226

1. out
2. back
3. by / in
4. on ... off
5. put ... out
6. up
7. up ... away / out
8. out ... back
9. up
10. on

PRACTICE 7, p. 227

1. up
2. over
3. after
4. up
5. out
6. down
7. up
8. out
9. off
10. up
11. out

PRACTICE 8, p. 228

1. back
2. up
3. out
4. over
5. on ... off
6. in ... out
7. on ... off
8. on ... off
9. up with
10. A: about / on
    B: along with
11. A: over ... in
    B: over